Britney Spears

Biography

Music, Life, and Strength

Anthony L Westbrook

CONTENT

Chapter 1

Raising a child in the South used to be about respecting one's parents and keeping one's mouth shut. Disagreement with a parent was never tolerated in my household. There was an agreement to remain silent no matter how awful things got, and if I didn't, there would be penalties.

The Bible states that your tongue is your sword.

My tongue and sword were my instruments for song.

I sang my entire childhood. On the drive to dance class, I sang along with the radio. I used to sing when I was depressed. Singing was spiritual to me.

I was born and raised in McComb, Mississippi, and now live in Kentwood, Louisiana, about 25 miles away.

We lived in a little brick house that had green-striped wallpaper and wood panelling. I used to go to Sonic, race go-karts, play basketball, and attend Parklane Academy, a Christian school.

Hearing our cleaner sing in the laundry room was the first time I was actually moved and felt shivers down my spine. I was always in charge of the family laundry and ironing, but when times were better financially, my mother would hire someone to assist her. The housekeeper sang gospel music, and it was like waking up on another planet. It's something I'll never forget.

My desire to sing has gotten stronger since then. Singing is a magical experience. I own who I am when I sing. I can communicate completely. When you sing, you stop saying "Hi, how are you..." You have the ability to say far more significant things. Singing transports me to a mystical realm where language no longer matters and anything is possible.

All I wanted was to be whisked away from the mundane and into a domain where I could express myself without hesitation. My mind was full of worries and dread when I was alone with my thoughts. Music silenced the cacophony, gave me confidence, and led me to a pure realm where I could express myself precisely how I wanted to be seen and heard. Singing transported me into the divine's presence. I was partially outside the world as long as I was singing. I'd be outside playing like any other kid, but my thoughts, feelings, and hopes were elsewhere.

I worked very hard to make everything appear the way I wanted it to. When I shot ridiculous music videos to Mariah Carey songs in my girlfriend's backyard, I took myself extremely seriously. I imagined myself to be a filmmaker by the age of eight. Nobody in my community seems to be doing anything like that. But I knew what I wanted to see in the world and worked hard to make it happen.

My father's world and my mother's world were diametrically opposed.

My mother's mother, Lilian "Lily" Portell, was from an exquisite, intelligent family in London, according to my mother. Everyone remarked on her unusual aura; her mother was British and her father was from the Mediterranean island of Malta. Her grandfather was a bookbinder. The entire family loved to sing and play music.

During WWII, Lily met an American soldier, my grandfather Barney Bridges, during a soldiers' dance. He was a general's driver who enjoyed driving quickly.

She was dismayed, however, when he brought her to America. She'd imagined a life similar to hers in London. As she drove from New Orleans to his dairy farm, she noticed how empty his world appeared through the glass of Barney's car. "Where are all the lights?" she asked her new spouse repeatedly.

I see Lily travelling through the Louisiana countryside at night, looking out into the darkness, understanding that her wide, lively, music-filled world of afternoon teas and London museums was going to turn little and hard. Instead of going to the movies or shopping for clothes, she would have to spend her time in the country cooking, cleaning, and milking cows.

So my grandma isolated herself, devoured books, grew obsessed with cleaning, and pined for London till the day she died. My relatives claimed that Barney didn't want Lily to return to London because he feared she wouldn't return.

My mother claimed Lily was so preoccupied with her own thoughts that she began clearing the table before everyone had finished eating.

All I knew was that my grandma was lovely, and I enjoyed imitating her British accent. Speaking with a British accent has always made me happy since it reminds me of my elegant grandmother. I wished I had her politeness and her beautiful voice.

Because Lily was wealthy, my mother, Lynne, her brother, Sonny, and her sister, Sandra, grew up with what you would call "money-money," especially in rural Louisiana. My mother attended Catholic school despite the fact that her parents were Protestant. She was stunning as a teen, with her black hair cut short. She always wore the tallest boots and the smallest skirts to school. She socialised with the town's gay men, who gave her rides on their motorcycles.

My father was obviously interested in her. My father was an incredible athlete, which was probably due in part to June forcing him to work so hard. People would go long distances to see him play basketball.

When my mother spotted him, she said, "Oh, who is this?"

According to all accounts, their relationship arose from mutual desire and a sense of adventure. But the honeymoon was over long before I arrived.

Chapter 2

My parents married and moved into a tiny house in Kentwood. My mother's relatives no longer supported her, thus my parents were impoverished. My parents were also young—my mother was twenty-one and my father was twenty-three. Bryan, my older brother, was born in 1977. They bought a little three-bedroom ranch house after leaving their previous small place.

My mother returned to school to become a teacher when Bryan was born. My father, who worked as a welder at oil refineries—hard jobs that could last a month or three—began to drink heavily, and it was soon taking its toll on the family.

Everything appeared to be tranquil for a time. My father quit welding and founded a building company. Then, after much effort, he established a gym business as well. Total Fitness was the name of the program, and it turned some of the guys in town, including my uncles, into bodybuilders. He ran it out of a separate studio area on our property, near to the home. An endless stream of muscular guys entered and exited the gym, flexing their muscles in the mirrors lit by fluorescent lights.

My father began to do exceptionally well. He became one of the wealthiest guys in our small town. My family hosted large crawfish boils in our garden. They had wild parties with all-night dancing.

My mother and her sister, my aunt Sandra, founded a daycare centre. My parents had a second child, me, to strengthen their marriage. On December 2, 1981, I was born. My mother never failed to remind me that she had been in terrible labour with me for twenty-one hours.

My family's women were my favourites. At the age of thirty-five, my aunt Sandra, who already had two sons, welcomed a surprise baby: my cousin Laura Lynne. Laura Lynne and I were like twins just a few months apart, and we were great friends. Laura Lynne was like a sister to me, and Sandra was like a second mother to me. She was incredibly supportive and proud of me.

Even though my grandma Jean died before I was born, I had the good fortune to meet her mother, my great-grandmother Lexie Pierce. Lexie was stunningly gorgeous, with a white, white face and red, red lipstick. She was a badass, and she became more so as she grew older. I was informed, and believed, that she had been married seven times. Seven! She obviously detested her son-in-law June, but once her daughter Jean died, she stayed and cared for my father and his siblings, as well as her great-grandchildren.

Lexie and I went to the movies one day. As we drove away from the video store, she collided with another car and became stuck in a hole. We couldn't leave. We needed a tow truck to come and get us. My mother was terrified by the accident. I wasn't permitted to see my great-grandmother after that.

"It wasn't even a bad accident!" I said to my mom. I begged Lexie to see me. My favourite person was her.

"No, I'm afraid she's getting senile," my mother responded. "It's not safe for you to be with her alone anymore."

I saw her at my place after that, but I couldn't get in the car with her or have sleepovers with her again. It was a devastating blow to me. I couldn't understand how being with someone I cared about could be dangerous.

Aside from spending time with Lexie, my favourite thing to do at that age was hide in cabinets. "Where's Britney now?" became a family joke. I always vanished at my aunt's house. Everyone would go on the hunt for me. Just as they were about to worry, they'd open a cabinet door and there I was.

I must have desired that they look for me. That was my thing for years—hiding.

I gained notice by hiding. I also like singing and dancing. I sang in our church choir and attended dance classes three nights a week and on Saturdays. Then I took gymnastics courses in Covington, Louisiana, an hour away. I could never get enough of dancing, singing, and acrobatics.

At primary school, I declared that I wanted to be a lawyer, but neighbours and teachers began to tell me that I was "Broadway bound," and I eventually accepted my identity as "the little entertainer."

My first dancing recital was when I was three, and I was four when I performed my first solo, "What Child Is This?" for a Christmas concert at my mother's daycare.

I wanted to be noticed as much as I wanted to hide. Both of these statements could be correct. I felt so small huddled in the cool darkness of a cabinet that I could vanish. But with everyone's attention on me, I transformed into someone who could dominate a room. I felt like anything was possible when wearing white tights and shouting out a tune.

Chapter 3

When I was four, I was sitting on the couch in our living room with my mom on one side and my friend Cindy on the other. Kentwood was like a soap opera town—there was constant drama. Cindy was telling my mother about the newest scandal as I was listening in and trying to keep up when the door burst open. I could tell something terrible had happened based on the boy's expression. My heart rate slowed.

My mother and I began running. The road had recently been repaved, and I was jogging barefoot on the scorching black tar.

"Ow! Ow! Ow!" With each step, I yelped. When I looked down at my feet, I noticed tar on them.

We eventually got to the field where my brother, Bryan, was playing with his neighbourhood buddies. They were attempting to mow some thick grass with their four-wheelers. Because they were idiots, this sounded like a terrific idea to them. They eventually collided because they couldn't see one other through the dense grass.

I must have seen everything, heard Bryan cry in agony and my mother scream in terror, but I have no recollection of any of it. I believe God made me black out so I wouldn't recall the anguish and worry, or the sight of my crushed brother's body.

He was transported to the hospital by helicopter.

Bryan was in a full body cast when I went to see him a few days later. He'd shattered practically every bone in his body, from what I could see. As a kid, the fact that he had to pee through a hole in the cast sealed the deal for me.

Another thing I couldn't help but notice was that the entire room was crammed with toys. My parents were so thankful he'd lived and so sorry for him that every day of his recovery felt like Christmas. My mother catered to my brother out of guilt. Even today, she defers to him. It's amazing how one short second can forever alter the dynamics of a family.

My brother and I grew closer as a result of the accident. Our friendship was developed as a result of my real recognition of his anguish. I wouldn't leave his side until he got home from the hospital. Every night, I slept next to him. Because he still had the full body cast, he couldn't sleep in his own bed. So he had a special bed, and they had to put a small mattress at the foot of it for me. I used to climb into his bed and just hold him.

I shared a bed with him for years after the cast came off. My brother had a rough childhood, even as a small child, because of the accident and how hard our father was on him. I wanted to make him feel better.

After years of this, my mother finally said to me, "Britney, you're almost in sixth grade now." You must begin sleeping by yourself!"

No, I said.

I was such a baby that I refused to sleep by myself. But she insisted, and I had no choice but to give in.

I learned to love having my own space after I started staying in my own room, but I stayed incredibly close to my brother. He adored me. And I adored him—I had the most charming, protective love for him. I didn't want him to be hurt again. I'd seen him go through too much already.

As my brother recovered, we became more involved in the community. Because it was a little town of only a couple thousand people, everyone came out to support the three major parades that took place each year: Mardi Gras, Fourth of July, and Christmas. The entire community was looking forward to them. People would be smiling and waving, leaving behind the drama of their life for a day to enjoy seeing their neighbours slowly pass by on Highway 38.

A group of us kids decided to decorate a golf cart and march it in the Mardi Gras parade one year. There were approximately eight kids in that golf cart, which was plainly far too many. There were three people on the bench seat, two on the sides holding on to the small roof, and one or two swinging from the back. It was so hefty that the cart's tires were nearly flat. I can't remember why we all wore nineteenth-century costumes. I was sitting on the laps of the older children in the front, waving to everyone. The trouble was that with so many kids in a golf cart, with its flat tires, the machine became difficult to control, and with all the laughing and waving and joyful energy... We barely struck the car ahead of us a few times, but it was enough to get us kicked out of the procession.

Chapter 4

My father's businesses began to crumble when he resumed heavy drinking.

The burden of not having money was exacerbated by my father's dramatic mood swings. I was especially afraid to get in the car with my father because he would chat to himself while driving. I couldn't make out what he was saying. He appeared to be lost in his own universe.

Even back then, I could see my father had reasons for wanting to bury himself in alcohol. Work was causing him stress. I can understand now that he was self-medicating after years of abuse at the hands of his father, June. But I had no understanding why he was so harsh on us at the time, why nothing we did seemed to be good enough for him.

The saddest part for me was that all I ever wanted was a father who would accept me for who I was—someone who would say, "I just love you." You have the ability to do anything right now. I'd still love you unconditionally."

My father was irresponsible, cold, and cruel to me, but he was even more so to Bryan. He was brutal in pushing him to do well in sports. Bryan's life was considerably more difficult than mine during those years since our father subjected him to the same rigorous routine June had imposed on him. Bryan was compelled to play basketball and football despite his physical limitations.

My father could also be abusive to my mother, although he was more of a drinker who would disappear for days at a time. To be honest, his departure was a favour to us. I liked it better when he wasn't there.

My mother would argue with him all night, which made his time at home extra unpleasant. He couldn't speak since he was so inebriated. I'm not sure he could even hear her. But we might be able to. Bryan and I were forced to bear the effects of her fury, which included being unable to sleep through the night. Her screams would reverberate throughout the house.

"Just feed him and go put him to bed!" I'd storm out into the living room in my nightgown. He's ill!"

She was battling with someone who wasn't even aware. But she refused to listen. I'd go back to bed, scowling at the ceiling, listening to her yell, cursing her in my heart.

Isn't it terrible? He was the one who was inebriated. He was the one whose alcoholism had caused us to be so impoverished. He was the one who had passed out on his chair. But she was the one who irritated me the most, because he was quiet in those moments. I was desperate to sleep, but she wouldn't stop talking.

Despite the nightly drama, my mother made our house a place where my friends wanted to hang out—at least when my father respected us enough to drink somewhere else. Everyone in the neighbourhood came over. For want of a better term, our house was the cool house. We had a tall bar with twelve chairs arranged around it. My mother was a typical young Southern mother, often gossiping and smoking cigarettes with her friends at the bar (she smoked Virginia Slims, the same smokes I currently smoke) or talking on the phone with them. I was dead to them all. The older kids would sit in the bar stools in front of the television and play video games. I was the youngest; I didn't know how to play video games, so I had to compete for the attention of the older kids.

Our home resembled a zoo. My mom was often rushing after Bryan when he was tiny, hopping over sofas attempting to grab him so she could swat him when he back-talked her.

I was always overjoyed, trying to grab the bigger kids' attention away from the screen in the living room or the adults to stop talking to each other in the kitchen.

"Britney, stop!" would shout at my mother. "We have visitors!" Just be courteous. Be on your best behaviour."

But I choose to ignore her. And I was always able to capture everyone's attention.

Chapter 5

I was little and quiet, but when I sang, I came alive, and I had enough gymnastics training to move effectively. I entered a local dance competition when I was five years old. My skill was a dance routine performed while wearing a top hat and twirling a cane. I won. My mother then began taking me to contests all around the region. I'm sporting the most outrageous outfits in previous photos and videos. I dressed like a Christmas present in my third-grade musical, wearing a loose purple T-shirt with a giant purple bow on top of my head. It was truly dreadful.

I worked my way up the talent circuit, eventually winning a regional competition in Baton Rouge. Before long, my parents had their sights set on bigger chances than what we might achieve by collecting prizes in school gymnasiums. They suggested we go when they read an announcement in the papers for an open call for The All New Mickey Mouse Club. We drove to Atlanta for eight hours. There were over 2,000 children present. I had to stand out, especially since we later discovered that they were only seeking for children above the age of ten.

When the casting director, Matt Casella, asked my age, I opened my lips to respond "Eight," then remembered the age-ten threshold and said, "Nine!" He gave me a suspicious glance.

I auditioned by singing "Sweet Georgia Brown" while performing a dance routine that included gymnastics flips.

Christina Aguilera, a girl from Pennsylvania, and I were told we didn't make the cut but that we were talented. Matt stated we'd be able to get on the show if we were older and more experienced. He suggested to my mother that we travel to New York City for work. He suggested we find an agent he respected who helped young actors get started in the theatre.

We did not leave right away. Instead, I stayed in Louisiana for approximately six months and started to work, serving tables at Lexie's seafood restaurant, Granny's Seafood and Deli, to help out.

My mother sent a video of me to Nancy Carson, the agent Matt had recommended. In the video, I sang "Shine On, Harvest Moon." It worked: she invited us to meet with her in New York.

We got back on the Amtrak and proceeded home after I sang for Nancy in her workplace twenty stories up in a building in Midtown Manhattan. A talent agency had officially signed me.

Jamie Lynn, my younger sister, was born not long after we returned to Louisiana. Laura Lynne and I spent hours in the playhouse pretending she was one of our dolls.

I was getting ready for a dance competition a few days after my mother returned home with the baby when she began acting strangely. She was hand-sewing a rip in my outfit, but she got up and threw it away while she was manipulating the needle and thread. She didn't appear to understand what she was doing. To be honest, the costume was a shambles, but I needed it to compete.

"Mama! Why did you throw my costume away?" I said.

Then there was blood all of a sudden. There was blood everywhere.

Something had not been correctly sewed up after she gave delivery. She was dripping with blood. I cried out for my father. "What's wrong with her?" I exclaimed. "What's wrong with her?"

Daddy arrived and drove her to the hospital. "Something cannot be wrong with my mom!" I yelled the entire journey.

I was nine years old. A river of blood gushing out of your mother would be upsetting for anyone, but it was horrific for a youngster that age. I'd never seen so much blood in my life.

When we arrived at the doctor's office, they had her mended in what seemed like two seconds. Nobody appeared really bothered. Postpartum haemorrhage appears to be rather common. But it stayed with me.

I'd constantly look to see if my mom was on the other side of the window, waiting for me to finish gymnastics class. It was a reflex that I had to perform in order to feel protected. But one day, when I went out the window to check in, she wasn't there. I became terrified. She'd gone. She has vanished! Perhaps indefinitely! I burst into tears. I knelt on my knees. You'd think someone had died if you saw me.

My teacher came running over to console me. "Honey, she's going to come back!" she exclaimed. "It's all right! She most likely went to Walmart!"

My mother had, in fact, done just that: she had gone to Walmart. But it was not acceptable. I couldn't bear the thought of her going. She never left that window during class again after seeing how unhappy I was when she returned. And she never left my side for the following few years.

I was a young girl with huge ambitions. I want to be a celebrity such as Madonna, Dolly Parton, or Whitney Houston. I had simpler ambitions as well, dreams that appeared even more difficult to fulfil and felt too ambitious to express aloud: I want my father to stop drinking. I'd like my mother to stop yelling. I want everything to be well.

With my family, anything might happen at any time. I had no authority there. Only while I was performing did I feel completely invincible. At least one thing was fully within my control as I stood in a Manhattan conference room in front of a woman who could make my fantasies come true.

Chapter 6

I was invited to be a participant on Star Search when I was ten years old.

At the first event, I sang a spirited rendition of a Judy Garland song called "I Don't Care." I received 3.75 stars. My opponent, an opera singer, received a 3.5. I moved on to the next round. The second show was taped later that day, and I was up against Marty Thomas, a twelve-year-old bolo-tie-wearing boy with a lot of hair spray in his hair. We were amicable, and we even played basketball before the show. I sang the Judds' "Love Can Build a Bridge," which I'd performed at my aunt's wedding the year before.

I received 3.75 once again. Marty received a perfect score of 4. Ed wished me well as I walked away after I smiled and hugged him gently. I kept it together until I got backstage, at which point I fell into tears. My mother then got me a hot fudge sundae.

I was offered a role as an understudy in Ruthless!, an off-Broadway musical inspired by The Bad Seed, All About Eve, Mame, and Gypsy. Tina Denmark, a psychotic child star, was the character I played. Tina's first hit was "Born to Entertain." It was really close to home. Natalie Portman, a promising young actress, was the other understudy.

While I was performing in the play, we rented a small apartment near my public school, the Professional Performing Arts School, for my mother, Jamie Lynn, and myself, and I took courses nearby at Broadway Dance Center. But I usually spent my time at the downtown Players Theatre.

In some ways, the experience was a confirmation, proof that I had the talent to make it in the theatrical world. However, it was a demanding schedule. I didn't have time to be a normal youngster or develop friends because I had to work virtually every day. There were two shows on Saturdays.

I also disliked being an understudy. Every night, I had to be at the theatre until as late as midnight in case I had to fill in for the main Tina, Laura Bell Bundy. She left after a few months, and I took over as leader, but I was exhausted.

By the time Christmas rolled around, I was desperate to get home—until I discovered I was slated to perform on Christmas Day. "Am I really going to do this for Christmas?" I questioned my mother, in tears. I glanced at our tiny apartment tree, picturing the robust evergreen we'd have in our living room in Kentwood.

In my little-girl thinking, I couldn't fathom why I'd want to do that—perform during the holidays. As a result, I left the show and went home.

The New York City theatre schedule was simply too demanding for me at the time. But one good thing came out of it: I learnt how to sing in a venue with poor acoustics. The audience is right alongside you—there are just 200 individuals in the room. To be honest, it's funny, but singing feels more electrifying in that atmosphere. The intimacy you feel with the members in the audience is unique. Their excitement energised me.

With that experience under my belt, I tried out for the Mickey Mouse Club again.

While waiting to hear about the Mickey Mouse Club in Kentwood, I became a basketball point guard at Parklane Academy. I was small for an eleven-year-old, but I could run the plays. People think I was a cheerleader, but I was never one. I dabbled in dancing on the side, but in school, I wanted to play ball, so I did despite my height. I wore a gigantic number 25 jersey that was far too big for me. I was a tiny mouse zipping around outside.

For a while, I had a crush on a fifteen or sixteen-year-old basketball player. He hit every three-point attempt and made it seem effortless. People would travel long distances to see him play, just as they had to see my father. He was good—not as brilliant as my father had been, but nonetheless a ball genius.

I was awestruck by him and my friends who were taller than me. My move was to grab the ball from an opponent player in mid-dribble, race down the court, and make a layup.

I like the rush of quickly weaving around the opposing team. The adrenaline of not having a script and the play being spontaneous and utterly unknown made me feel so alive. No one noticed me coming because I was so small and charming.

It wasn't the same as being onstage in New York City, but it seemed like the next best thing under the bright lights of the court, waiting for the sound of applause.

Chapter 7

My second audition for the Mickey Mouse Club resulted in a booking. Matt, the pleasant casting director who had suggested my mother to our agency, Nancy, thought I was ready.

Being in the program was like boot camp for the entertainment industry: there were long dance rehearsals, singing lessons, acting workshops, recording studio time, and school in between. The Mouseketeers rapidly splintered into cliques, separated by the dressing rooms we shared: Christina Aguilera and I were the younger kids, sharing a dressing room with another girl, Nikki DeLoach. We looked up to the older kids, like Keri Russell, Ryan Gosling, and Tony Lucca, who I thought was quite attractive. And I rapidly became acquainted with a young man named Justin Timberlake.

The only downer was learning that my grandmother Lily had died not long into filming. She perished in the pool while swimming, maybe as a result of a heart attack or stroke. We couldn't afford to go home for Justin's funeral, but Lynn Harless, Justin's generous mother, agreed to lend us the plane ticket. It was something that a family would do, and the children and adults on that show were like family.

The Mickey Mouse Club was a fantastic experience that got my feet wet in the world of television. Performing on that show sparked my interest. I knew then that I wanted to do what I did there—sing and dance.

Back at home, I returned to Parklane, settling into typical adolescent life—or the closest thing to "normal" that my family allowed.

Trips to the beach with my sister were some of my favourite times with my parents. I'd sip a little teeny White Russian while we drove. The drink tasted like ice cream to me. That was my slice of heaven when it had just the right amount of shaved ice, cream, and sugar, but not too much alcohol.

I began drinking with my mother and smoking with my pals by the age of thirteen. I smoked my first cigarette at the home of one of my "bad" friends. All of my other pals were nerds, but this one was popular: her sister was a senior, she always wore the nicest makeup, and guys flocked to her.

I did a decent job of concealing my habit from my mother, but one day she had me drive us home from the store along the long road that led to our house—I started driving at thirteen, too—when she suddenly began sniffing the air.

"I smell smoke!" exclaimed her. "Have you been smoking?"

She quickly snatched one of my hands off the steering wheel and drew it to her to smell. I lost control of the steering wheel as she did this, and the car spun off the road. Everything seemed to be happening in slow motion. When I turned around, I noticed Jamie Lynn pressed backward into the seat: she was wearing a seat belt but wasn't in a car seat. I kept thinking, We're going to die, as we spun what felt like extremely slowly. We're going to die. We're going to die.

Then, bang! The car's buttocks collided with a telephone pole.

It was a miracle that we hit so hard. We would have gone through the windshield if we had hit the pole while moving ahead. My mother stepped out of the car and began yelling—at me for crashing, at cars passing by for assistance, and at the universe for allowing this to happen.

Fortunately, no one was injured. We all got up and walked away. Even better, my mother had forgotten about how she had caught me smoking. Is smoking in my adolescence a crime? Whatever. We were on the verge of death! She never mentioned it again after that.

I liked a lot of the males in my brother's group that year. Bryan was a funny kid—weird in the greatest way. But as a senior, he rose to become the school's monarch, a total badass.

During his senior year, I began dating his closest buddy and lost my virginity to him.

I was in ninth school, and the guy was seventeen. My involvement with him took up a lot of my time. I would arrive at school at seven a.m. as usual, then leave at lunchtime, around one p.m., to spend the afternoon with him. Then he'd drive me back just as school was ending. I'd just hop on the bus and go home as if nothing had occurred.

My mother eventually received a call from the school office; I'd missed seventeen days and would have to make them up.

The age difference between me and that person was plainly enormous—now it seems outrageous—and my protective older brother began to despise him. Bryan spotted me sneaking out to visit his friend and informed our parents. As punishment, I had to wander around the neighbourhood with a bucket all day, cleaning up garbage like a highway prisoner. Bryan followed me about, snapping pictures of me picking up trash as I was crying.

Aside from those instances, there was something so sweetly typical about that time in my life: going to homecoming and prom, driving around our small town, and going to the movies.

But, in reality, I missed performing. My mother had contacted a lawyer she'd met on my audition circuit, Larry Rudolph, whom she would occasionally call for business assistance. He suggested I make a demo after she emailed him footage of me singing. He had a song called "Today" that Toni Braxton had recorded for her second album but had left on the editing room floor. He sent me the song, which I learnt before recording it in a studio an hour and a half away in New Orleans. This would be the demo I'd use to get my foot in the door at record labels.

At the same time, Justin and another Mouseketeer, JC Chasez, were members of the newly formed boy band NSYNC. Another castmate, Nikki, with whom I'd shared that dressing room, was planning to join a girl group, but after consulting with my mother, we opted to go solo instead.

Larry played the demo for some executives in New York who expressed interest in seeing what I could do. So I put on my tiny heels and pretty little outfit and went back to New York.

I had attempted to return to being a normal adolescent, but it had failed. I was still looking for something more.

Chapter 8

Who exactly is this man? I pondered. I'm not sure, but I like his workplace and his dog a lot. He was simply a small old man, but he was full of vitality. I guessed he was around 65 years old (he was actually in his fifties).

He had a three-story office that was really imposing. And there was a teacup terrier in the office—a breed of dog I had no idea existed—that was, I swear to God, the tiniest, most adorable creature. I felt like I was entering a parallel universe when I came in and saw that office and that dog. Everything shifted into a new dimension. I walked into a fantastic dream.

"Hi, Britney!" he exclaimed, virtually shaking with excitement. "How are ya?"

He pretended to be a member of some great secret group. He spoke with a South African accent that made him sound like a character from an old movie. I'd never heard somebody speak like that in real life.

He allowed me to pick up his dog. I couldn't stop smiling as I carried the tiny animal in my arms and gazed around the massive workplace. My dreams took off at that precise moment.

Other than the demo, I hadn't recorded anything. I was just going to see these guys Larry had suggested I speak with. I was aware that I was supposed to perform a song for record label executives. And I knew I wanted to be around that guy more, and that the way he was influenced the way I wanted to be. I wouldn't be surprised if he was my uncle in another life. I wanted to know him forever.

Clive immediately signed me. So, at the age of fifteen, I signed a recording contract with Jive Records.

The booth where I sang was underneath. When you're inside, all you can hear is yourself singing. That was something I did for months. I didn't leave the booth.

Things were coming together for my debut record about a year into my tenure in New Jersey. Then one of the execs said to me, "You need to meet this Swedish producer." He's fantastic. He composes catchy music."

"All right," I replied. "Who has he worked with?"

I'm not sure how I knew to ask that question, given my inexperience, but I'd begun to have distinct notions about how I wanted to sound. I also conducted some research and discovered that at the time, he'd written songs for the Backstreet Boys, Robyn, and Bryan Adams.

"Yes," I said. "Let's do it."

Max Martin went to New York for a dinner meeting with only me and him, no aides or label officials present. Despite the fact that I was typically accompanied by handlers due to my age, they wanted me to meet him alone in this situation. As we sat, a waiter approached and asked, "How may I assist you?"

A candle accidentally flipped over, igniting the entire table.

We were in one of New York City's most expensive restaurants, and our table had suddenly turned into a wall of fire—from "How may I assist you?" to a flame wall in less than a second.

Max and I exchanged horrified looks. "Should we leave now?" he asked.

He was a wizard. And we began to collaborate.

I flew to Sweden to record songs, but the difference between there and New Jersey was barely discernible: I was just in another booth.

"Do you want some coffee?" Felicia would ask. Let's go get some fresh air!"

I'd shake her off. I laboured for hours on end. My work ethic was excellent. I'd never come out. You wouldn't hear from me for days if you knew who I was back then. I would spend as much time as I could in the studio. If someone wanted to leave, I'd tell them, "I wasn't perfect."

I was listening to Soft Cell's "Tainted Love" the night before we recorded "... Baby One More Time" and fell in love with that sound. I stayed up late to arrive at the studio weary and with my voice fried. It was successful. When I sang, it came out gravelly, sounding more mature and sexier.

I became obsessed with the recording once I realised what was going on. And Max was attentive. He understood what I meant when I stated I wanted more R&B in my voice and less plain pop, and he made it happen.

When all of the songs were finished, someone said, "What else can you do?" "Do you want to dance right now?"

"Do I want to dance?" I asked. I certainly do!"

Chapter 9

The label approached me with an idea for a video for "... Baby One More Time" in which I would portray a futuristic astronaut. The mock-up I saw depicted me as a Power Ranger. That image didn't resonate with me, and I suspected my audience wouldn't either. I told the label executives that I felt people would want to witness my friends and me sitting in school, bored, and then starting dancing as soon as the bell rang.

Beginning in the summer, Jive sent me on a mall tour—to around twenty-six malls! That type of promotion is not enjoyable. Nobody knew who I was at the time. I had to try to sell myself to people who were uninterested in me.

My demeanour was genuine—it wasn't an act. I had no idea what I was doing. I'd just say, "Hey, hello!" My music is fantastic! You have to look into it!"

Before the video, not many people knew what I looked like. However, by the end of September, the song was being played on the radio. On October 23, 1998, I was sixteen years old when the single "... Baby One More Time" was released. The video was released the next month, and I was suddenly known everywhere I went. The album was released on January 12, 1999, and it soon sold over ten million copies. In the United States, I debuted at number one on the Billboard 200 list. I was the first woman to have a number one single and album launch at the same time. I was overjoyed. And I could feel my life opening up. I no longer had to perform at shopping malls.

Things were moving quickly. I toured aboard tour buses with NSYNC, including my old Mickey Mouse Club pal Justin Timberlake. My dancers, Felicia, or one of my two managers, Larry Rudolph and Johnny Wright, were constantly with me. Big Rob, a security guard I hired, was incredibly nice to me.

On MTV's Total Request Live, I became a regular. Rolling Stone brought David LaChapelle to Louisiana to photograph me for the April cover story, "Inside the Heart, Mind, & Bedroom of a Teen Dream." The images were contentious when they were published since the cover shot of me in my underwear holding a Teletubby highlighted how young I was. My mother was apprehensive, but I was determined to work with David LaChapelle again.

Every day was different. I was meeting a lot of interesting folks! I met singer-songwriter Paula Cole at a New York party shortly after "Baby" was released. She was roughly fourteen years my senior. Oh my God, I admired her so much—at first, just because of her appearance. She was the tiniest thing, with the most curly brown hair cascading down her back. I had no notion who she was, only that she was stunning, with an extraordinary look and energy.

Years later, I discovered she was also the vocalist of songs I adored. When I initially heard her voice, I assumed she didn't look anything like she did. When she put her angelic face to her super-dirty words on "Feelin' Love," and her petite body with the strength of her voice on "I Don't Want to Wait," I learned how powerful it can be when women defy expectations.

Chapter 10

The intention was for me to perform "I'm a Slave 4 U" at the 2001 MTV Video Music Awards in September, with a snake as a prop. It's become an iconic moment in the history of the VMAs, but it was far scarier than it appeared.

I first saw the snake when it was delivered to a small back chamber of the Metropolitan Opera House in Manhattan, where we would be performing the play. The girl who gave it over was even smaller than me—she appeared to be extremely young and had blond hair. I couldn't believe they didn't have a large guy in charge—"You're letting us two little munchkins handle this huge snake?" I thought.

But there we were, and there was no turning back: she hoisted the snake and wrapped it over my head and shoulders. To be honest, I was terrified—that snake was large, yellow and white, crinkly, and disgusting. It was fine because the girl who handed it to me, as well as a snake handler and a slew of other people, were present.

But everything changed when I had to perform the song onstage with the snake. Onstage, I'm in performance mode: I'm dressed up and there's no one else except me. When the little munchkin came to me again and brought me the gigantic snake, all I knew was to look down because I was afraid if I looked up and caught its eye, it would kill me.

In my brain, I was telling myself, "Just perform, just use your legs, just perform." Nobody knows, however, that as I was singing, the snake brought its head right up to my face and began hissing at me. You didn't see that shot on TV, but did you see it in real life? I was thinking to myself, "Are you serious right now?" The tongue of the fucking goddamn snake is flicking out at me. Right. Now. Thank God, I finally got to the part when I handed it back.

The next night, just days before September 11, I performed a duet of "The Way You Make Me Feel" with Michael Jackson to commemorate his solo career's 30th anniversary at Madison Square Garden in New York City. I prowled around the stage in my heels. The audience erupted. At one point, it seemed like the entire crowd of 20,000 was singing along with us.

Pepsi commissioned me to create advertisements for them. In "The Joy of Pepsi," I began as a delivery driver and ended up in a big dance routine. In "Now and Then," I got to dress up in gorgeous costumes from different eras. For the 1980s portion, I dressed up like Robert Palmer and sang "Simply Irresistible." I was in hair and makeup for four hours, and they still couldn't make me look like a man. In the fifties, however, I enjoyed dancing at the drive-in. My hair was like Betty Boop's. Working in all of those diverse genres, I was astounded by how well-thought-out those commercials were.

Crossroads, written by Shonda Rhimes and directed by Tamra Davis, was my debut film. We shot it in March 2001, around the time I was finishing up my album Britney. I played Lucy Wagner, a "good girl" in the film. It wasn't an easy process for me. My issue was not with any of the people engaged in the production, but with what acting did to my head. I believe I began Method acting, but I didn't know how to break out of my persona. I truly transformed into this other person. Some people practise Method acting, but they are usually conscious that they are doing it. But there was no divide between us.

It's awful to admit, but it's as if a cloud or something came over me and I just became Lucy. When the camera turned on, I became her, and I couldn't tell when the camera was on and when it wasn't. That may appear ridiculous, yet that is the truth. That's how serious I took it. I took it seriously enough that Justin asked, "Why are you walking like that? "What is your name?"

All I can say is that Lucy was a sweet child who wrote poems about how she was "not a girl, not yet a woman," and not a serial killer.

I ended up walking differently, carrying myself differently, and speaking differently as a result. For months, I pretended to be someone else while filming Crossroads. I'm sure the females I shot that movie with still think she's a touch... weird. They were correct in their assessment.

Like the character, I was a baby. I should've acted like myself on video. But I was so eager to do a good job that I kept attempting to delve into this character's backstory. I'd been myself my entire life and wanted to try something new! I should have realised it was a teen road movie. It isn't that deep. Honestly, just have fun. After the movie was finished, one of my girlfriends from a bar in LA came to see me. We went shopping at CVS. I swear to God, I stepped into the store, and as I talked to her while we shopped, I finally realised who I was. When I went outdoors again, the movie's magic had been broken. It was bizarre. My small spirit reappeared in my body. That trip to the makeup store with a buddy seemed like waving a magic wand.

Then I became enraged.

Oh my God, what have I been doing for the past few months? What exactly was I?

That was basically the start and conclusion of my acting career, and I was relieved. The Notebook casting came down to me and Rachel McAdams, and while reconnecting with Ryan Gosling after our time on the Mickey Mouse Club would have been wonderful, I'm glad I didn't do it. If I had, instead of working on my record In the Zone, I would have spent my days and nights dressing up as a 1940s heiress.

I'm sure a big part of the problem was that it was my first time acting. I'm sure there are folks in the acting industry who have struggled to separate themselves from a character. However, I believe they maintain perspective. I hope I never have to deal with that occupational hazard again. Being half yourself and half a fictional character is a bad way to live. After a while, you're not sure what's real.

Chapter 11

My fourth and favourite tour was the Dream Within a Dream Tour, which took place shortly after the release of my album Britney in the fall of 2001. Every night onstage, I had to combat a mirror version of myself, which felt like a metaphor for something. However, such a mirror act was only for one song. There was even some flying! And there's an Egyptian barge! And there's a jungle! Lasers! Snow!

They were astute in their presentation of me as a celebrity, and I know I owe them. They admired me as an artist because of how they captured me. That tour's creators were outstanding. It was by far my favourite tour.

It was just what we had all hoped for. I had worked so hard to get there. I'd done small tours before Baby was published, but the Baby tour was the first time I got to see a large crowd. I recall thinking, "Wow, I'm somebody now." Then Oops! grew in size, and by the time I completed the Dream Within a Dream Tour, everything was magical.

By the spring of 2002, I'd hosted SNL twice, first as a butter churn girl at a colonial reenactment museum alongside Jimmy Fallon and Rachel Dratch, and then as Barbie's younger sister, Skipper, alongside Amy Poehler as Barbie. In the same broadcast, I was the youngest person to host and perform as a musical guest.

I was asked if I wanted to be in a movie musical around that time. I wasn't sure if I wanted to act again after Crossroads, but this one persuaded me. It was the city of Chicago.

Executives from the production approached me at a performance location and asked if I wanted to do it. I'd turned down three or four films because I was so focused on the stage show. I didn't want to be taken away from the music. I was content with what I was doing.

In my personal life, I was overjoyed. Justin and I shared an apartment in Orlando. We shared a lovely, light-filled two-story home with a tile roof and a pool in the backyard. Even though we were both working a lot, we tried to spend as much time as we could at home together. I always returned every couple months so Justin and I could spend two weeks, sometimes even two months, together. That was our starting point.

That was a happy period in my life. I was head over heels in love with Justin. I'm not sure if love is different when you're younger, but what Justin and I shared was extraordinary. He wouldn't even have to say or do anything for me to be attracted to him.

To be honest, I thought it was a joke at first. I didn't believe my stylist would do it, and I certainly didn't think Justin would do it with me. They both, however, went all in.

Justin's all-denim costume, complete with a denim hat to match his denim jacket and denim leggings, was delivered by the stylist. I was surprised when he put it on. So, we're actually doing this!

Justin and I were constantly attending events together. We had a lot of fun at the Teen Choice Awards, and we frequently colour-coordinated our clothes. But we blew it up with the matching denim. That night, my corset had me squeezed in so tightly beneath my denim gown that I was on the verge of collapsing.

I get that it was tacky, but it was also fairly wonderful in its own right, and I love seeing it parodied as a Halloween costume. I've heard Justin get chastised for his appearance. On a podcast, he joked, "You do a lot of things when you're young and in love." That is completely correct. We were ecstatic, and our clothing reflected that.

I knew Justin had cheated on me a handful of times during our relationship. I let it go because I was so captivated and in love, even though the tabloids seemed determined to rub it in my face. When

NSYNC visited London in 2000, photographers caught him in a car with one of the All Saints females. But I didn't say anything. We'd just been together for a year at the time.

For years, I had only had eyes for Justin, with one exception, which I disclosed to him. That night was written off as something that happens when you're as young as we were, and Justin and I moved on and remained together. I assumed we'd be together for the rest of our lives. I was hoping we would be.

I became pregnant with Justin's baby when we were dating. It was unexpected, but it was hardly a tragedy in my opinion. Justin was my absolute favourite. I always imagined us having a family one day. This would just be far sooner than I had anticipated. After all, what was done was done.

But Justin was displeased with the pregnancy. He stated we weren't ready for a baby and that we were far too young.

I could see what you were saying. I mean, I kind of got it. I didn't think I had much of a choice if he didn't want to be a father. I wouldn't want to force him to do something he didn't want to do. Our friendship was far too crucial to me. So, even though I'm sure people will detest me for it, I agreed not to have the baby.

Abortion was not something I would have chosen for myself, but given the circumstances, it is what we did.

I'm not sure if that was the best decision. I would never have done it if it had been up to me alone. Despite this, Justin was adamant that he did not want to be a father.

We also agreed on something that, in retrospect, was, in my opinion, incorrect: I should not go to a doctor or a hospital to have the abortion. It was critical that no one knew about the pregnancy or the abortion, so everything had to be done at home.

We didn't even notify my family. Apart from Justin and me, the only other person who knew was Felicia, who was always willing to assist me. Someone said to me, "It might hurt a little bit, but you'll be fine."

I took the pills on the specified day, with only Felicia and Justin there. I soon began to have terrible cramping. I ran into the bathroom and stayed there for hours, sobbing and screaming on the floor. They should have numbed me with something, I reasoned. I desired some form of anaesthetic. I needed to see a doctor. I was terrified. I laid there wondering if I would die.

I can't even begin to convey how awful it was. The agony was unbearable. I crouched down on my knees, gripping the toilet. I couldn't move for a long time. It's still one of the most agonising things I've ever gone through in my life.

Nonetheless, they did not transport me to the hospital. Justin entered the bathroom and joined me on the floor. He felt music could help at some time, so he got his guitar and lay down with me, strumming it.

I sobbed and cried till it was all over. It took hours, and I don't recall how it finished, but I remember the pain and anxiety twenty years later.

I was messed up for a while after that, especially because I still loved Justin so much. It was absurd how much I liked him, and it was unfortunate for me.

I should have predicted the breakup, but I didn't.

Chapter 12

Even though I didn't want to play, I had tour dates left in my contract, so I went back out to finish them. I just wanted to get off the road: To have the entire day and night to myself. To stroll out onto the Santa Monica Pier, breathe in the salt air, listen to the roller coaster rattle, and gaze out at the sea. Instead, every day was a struggle. Fill up. Load up. Check the volume. Photographic session. "What town are we even in?" he wonders.

I used to enjoy the Dream Within a Dream Tour, but it had turned into a chore. I was exhausted both mentally and physically. I wanted to turn everything off. I'd started thinking about owning a small shop on Venice Beach with Felicia and retiring from show business entirely. With the benefit of hindsight, I can see that I didn't give myself enough time to recover from Justin's split.

We headed south in late July 2002, near the end of the trip, to perform in Mexico City. But getting there was nearly impossible.

We were riding in vans, and after crossing the border, we came to a halt. We'd been stopped by a group of men with the largest firearms I'd ever seen. I was afraid, like if we were being ambushed. It didn't make sense to me, but all I knew was that we were surrounded by these enraged men. Everyone in my van was tense; I had security, but who knew what would happen? After what seemed like an eternity, there appeared to be some kind of peace discussions taking place, as if in a movie. It's still a mystery to me what transpired, but we were eventually allowed to continue, and we got to play in front of 50,000 people (albeit the second gig, the next day, had to be cancelled halfway through due to a major thunderstorm).

That storm-cancelled event was the final date of the Dream Within a Dream Tour, but when I told people after the tour that I needed to recuperate, they were all anxious. When you're successful at something, there's a lot of pressure to continue doing it even if you're no longer enjoying it. And, as I quickly discovered, you can't go home again.

Back in Louisiana, I did an interview with People magazine for reasons that seemed absurd to me: I wasn't marketing anything, but my team thought I should show that I was doing well and "just taking a little break."

The photographer photographed me both outside and inside, with the dogs and my mother on the couch. They made me empty my purse to prove I wasn't carrying narcotics or cigarettes: all they discovered were Juicy Fruit gum, vanilla perfume, mints, and a small vial of St. John's wort. "My daughter is doing beautifully," my mother assured the reporter. "She's never, ever been close to a breakdown."

Part of what made that time so tough was that Justin's family was the only genuine, loving family I had. I would only spend holidays with his family. I knew his grandmother and grandfather, and I adored them. They reminded me of home. My mother would come out and visit us every now and again, but she was never the person I went home to.

I was always the worker bee. I hadn't been paying attention to what was going on in Kentwood while I was doing my thing on the road with Felicia. But when I returned home, I noticed how things had changed. My mother would bring Jamie Lynn small chocolate milkshakes as she watched TV. The girl clearly dominated the roost.

Life in Louisiana had slipped away from me. I didn't know who to talk to. Going through that breakup, returning home, and realising how much I didn't fit in anywhere anymore, I understood I was technically maturing, becoming a woman. And yet, in my imagination, it was almost as if I went backwards and became younger at the same time. Have you ever watched the film The

Curious Case of Benjamin Button? That's exactly how I felt. That year, as I became more vulnerable, I began to feel like a child again.

Chapter 13

In order to regain my confidence, I travelled to Milan in September 2002 to see Donatella Versace. That journey re-energized me, reminding me that there was still fun to be had in the world. We drank fantastic wine and ate fantastic food. Donatella was an engaging host. I was hopeful that things would start to improve from there.

She had asked me to one of her runway presentations in Italy. Donatella clothed me in a stunning dazzling rainbow gown. I was meant to sing, but I didn't feel like it, so after some posing, Donatella said we could take it easy. She played my rendition of Joan Jett's "I Love Rock 'n' Roll," I introduced myself to the models, and we were done.

Then it was time to celebrate. Donatella is notorious for throwing extravagant parties, and this was no exception. I remember seeing Lenny Kravitz and other amazing individuals there. That party was truly the first time I put myself out there following Justin's breakup—on my own, naïve.

During the party, I observed a guy and thought he was really cute. He appeared to be Brazilian: black hair, beautiful, smoking a blunt—your standard bad boy. He wasn't like the LA actor types I'd met before; he was more like a real man, the kind of man you'd have a one-night stand with. He was only for sex.

He was talking to these two girls when I first noticed him, but I could tell he wanted to talk to me.

We eventually started communicating, and I planned to meet him for drinks at my hotel. We drove to my car, but he did something that completely turned me off—I honestly can't remember what it was. But there was one small detail that irked me, so I urged the driver to pull over and, without saying anything, I kicked the person out on the side of the road and left him there.

Now that I'm a mother, I'd never do something like that—I'd say, "I'll drop you off at this location at this time..." But it was instinct at the time, when I was twenty years old. I'd made a mistake by letting this man into my automobile, so I threw him out.

Justin told everyone that he and I had a sexual relationship, which some have said painted me as not only a cheating slut but also a liar and hypocrite. Because I had so many adolescent followers, my management and publicity agents had long sought to depict me as an everlasting virgin—despite the fact that Justin and I had been living together and having sex since I was fourteen.

Was I upset because he "outed" me as sexually active? No. To be honest, I liked how Justin said that. Why did my management strive so hard to portray me as a young-girl virgin far into my twenties? Who cared whether I'd had sex or not?

I'd enjoyed it when Oprah said on her show that my sexuality was none of their concern, and that when it came to virginity, "you don't need a world announcement if you change your mind."

Yes, I contributed to that portrayal as a teenager because everyone was making such a huge deal about it. But, when you think about it, it was very dumb of people to describe my physique in that way, to point to me and say, "Look! A virgin!" It's none of your business. And it pulled the spotlight away from me as a musician and performer. I worked extremely hard on my music and performance acts. But the only questions some reporters had for me were whether or not my breasts were real (they were) and whether or not my hymen was intact.

Justin's admission to everyone that we'd had a sexual relationship broke the ice and ensured that I never had to come out as a non-virgin. His mentioning our sex never upset me, and I've defended him to some who have attacked him for doing so. "That's so rude!" people have commented regarding his sexual comments about me. But I enjoyed it. When he stated that, I heard him say, "She's a woman." She is not a virgin. "Be quiet."

I'd always had a guilty conscience, a lot of shame, and a sense that my family felt I was just plain awful as a kid. The despair and loneliness that would strike me felt somehow my fault, as if I deserved misfortune and poor luck. I knew the truth about our relationship wasn't what was being depicted, but I still assumed that if I was suffering, it was because I deserved it. I'd undoubtedly done horrible things along the way. Because I believe in karma, I imagine that when awful things happen, it's just the law of karma catching up with me.

I've always been quite sensitive. Even though I'm thousands of miles away, I can sense what folks in Nebraska are feeling. Women's cycles sometimes coincide; I feel like my emotions are always in sync with those around me. I'm not sure what hippie term to use—cosmic consciousness, intuition, psychic connection. All I know is that I can completely sense other people's energy. I can't help but notice it.

You could be thinking to yourself at this time, "Oh my God, is she really going to talk about this New Age stuff?"

Just one more minute.

Because the point is, I was sensitive, young, and still reeling from the abortion and breakup; I didn't handle things well. Justin framed our time together with me as the bad person, and I bought into it, so I've felt cursed ever since.

And yet, if it were true, if I had so much negative karma, it might be up to me—as an adult, as a woman—to reverse my luck, to bring myself good fortune.

I couldn't take it any longer and fled to Arizona with a partner. That girlfriend was dating Justin's best buddy, and we'd all split up around the same time, so we decided to take a road trip to get away from it all. We found each other and decided to leave everything behind.

My buddy was heartbroken, too, given what she'd gone through, so we chatted a lot, beside ourselves with loss and loneliness, and I was grateful for her friendship.

The sky above us was full of stars as we sped through the desert in a convertible with the top down and the wind in our hair—no music playing, just the sound of the night blasting past us.

An unsettling feeling fell over me as we peered out at the road in front of us. I'd been going so quickly for so long that I couldn't catch my breath. Something flooded me just now: a tremendous beauty, otherworldly and humbling. I looked across to my companion, unsure whether I should say anything. But what could I possibly say? "Do you believe in aliens?" So I kept quiet and sat with the feeling for a long time.

Then I heard her voice above the din of the wind.

"Do you feel that?" she inquired. She gave me a look. "What is that?"

Whatever it was, she sensed it as well.

I took her hand in mine and squeezed it tightly.

Rumi, the poet, says that the wound is where the light enters you. That is something I have always believed. We felt what we felt that night in Arizona because we needed it at the time. We were both spiritually open and spiritually raw. It demonstrated that there was more to life than what we could see—call it God, a higher power, or a paranormal experience. Whatever it was, it was genuine enough for us to share the experience. I didn't want to bring it up with my pal at first since I felt embarrassed. I was afraid she'd think I'd gone insane.

I've been frightened to speak up so many times because I was terrified someone would think I was insane. But I had to learn that lesson the hard way. Even if it worries you, you must express what you are experiencing. You must convey your story. You must raise your voice.

That night, when I was lost and felt God in the wilderness, I still had a lot to learn. But I knew I wasn't going to let the darkness engulf me. Even in the darkest night, there is plenty of light.

Chapter 14

According to what I heard, Justin slept with six or seven different girls in the weeks following our official breakup. He was Justin Timberlake, after all. This was his first solo trip. He was every girl's fantasy. I was madly in love with him. I could see why people were so taken with him.

I decided that if Justin was going to date, I should try to do the same. I hadn't dated in a long time, having been devastated and on tour. That winter, I saw a handsome guy, and a club promoter buddy told me I had good taste.

We ended up fighting for two weeks. We were all over each other, battling so furiously that it felt like we were in a street battle.

During our enjoyable time together, he took me to the premiere of The Recruit, a spy thriller starring Al Pacino. I was overjoyed when he asked me to accompany him. I was dressed in a PJ top. I believed it was a real shirt because it had little studs on it, but after seeing the images, I realised: Yeah, I certainly wore a full-fledged pyjama top to Colin Farrell's premiere.

I was overjoyed to be there for the premiere. Colin's entire family was present, and they were all really kind.

I tried to convince myself, like I had before when I was too attached to a man, that it wasn't a huge problem, that we were just having fun, that in this case I was vulnerable because I wasn't over Justin yet. But for a tiny minute, I thought there could be something there.

My romantic disappointments were only one factor in how alienated I grew. I was constantly self-conscious.

While the news about me was frequently unfavourable, the entertainment press was replete with glowing reports about Justin and Christina Aguilera. Justin was half-naked on the cover of Rolling Stone. Christina appeared on the cover of Blender dressed as an Old West madam. They were on the cover of Rolling Stone, him in a black tank top and gorgeous eyes, her peering out at the camera in a lace-up black blouse. She said in that story that she thought Justin and I should get back together, which was odd given how critical she'd been elsewhere.

It hurt to see individuals I'd known for so long talk negatively about me in the press. Even if they weren't intentionally harsh, it felt like they were rubbing salt in the wound. Why was it so simple for everyone to forget that I was a human being, vulnerable enough for these headlines to sting?

I only went out on rare occasions. One night, I dressed up in a $129 Bebe dress and high heels and went to a hot underground club with low ceilings and red walls with my cousin. My first time consuming marijuana, I took a couple hits from a joint. Later, I walked all the way home to soak in the sights of the city, breaking one of my heels in the process. When I arrived at my flat, I went to my terrace and spent hours stargazing. I felt one with New York at that time.

Madonna was one of my few guests during that bizarre, surreal time. She walked into the room and, of course, she immediately owned it. I recall thinking, "This is Madonna's room now." She was stunningly attractive and emanated strength and confidence. She stepped straight to the window and said, "Nice view."

"Yeah, it's a nice view, I guess," he replied.

Madonna's unwavering confidence let me see my position with new eyes. I believe she had an innate grasp of what I was going through. I needed some direction at the moment. I was perplexed about my life. She attempted to coach me.

She performed a red-string ceremony with me at one time to

introduce me into Kabbalah, and she gave me a trunk full of Zohar volumes to pray with. I tattooed a Hebrew term that means one of God's seventy-two names at the base of my neck. Some Kabbalists see it as healing, which is what I was still attempting to achieve.

Madonna had a positive influence on me in many ways. She advised me to make time for my soul, and I attempted to do so. She exemplified the kind of strength I needed to witness. There were so many various ways to be a woman in the industry: you could be a diva, a professional, or just "nice." I had always worked so hard to please—my parents, the audience, everyone.

My mother must have instilled in me a sense of powerlessness. I witnessed how my sister and father handled her and how she just accepted it. I adopted that model early in my career and became passive. I wish I'd had a badass bitch mentor back then so I could've learnt how to do that sooner. If I could go back in time, I would attempt to be my own parent, partner, and advocate, much like Madonna. She had faced sexism and bullying from the public and the industry, as well as being embarrassed for her sexuality on numerous occasions, but she had always triumphed.

I got an idea for a collaboration while we were rehearsing for the VMAs. My crew and I were seated on silver metal folding chairs in the Culver City studio, discussing how the record company was lukewarm on my new song "Me Against the Music"—a tune I liked. I'd just done "I'm a Slave 4 U" on my previous record, and my label's owner, Barry Weiss, wanted more songs like that. But I was pushing for "Me Against the Music" with all my might.

"Then what if we do a feature on it?" I said. Because of the incident that inspired it, a song can become a major hit. I reasoned that if we could find someone to sing on the tune, we could make a tale out of it.

"Who do you want to feature?" my boss said.

"Her!" I exclaimed, motioning across the room to Madonna. "Let's get her on the song."

"Holy shit," he exclaimed. "Yeah—that'd work." We agreed that instead of asking through her team, I would ask her directly.

So I went to see Madonna. "Let's talk," I suggested. I told her how much pleasure it would be to sing the song with her and how I thought we could help each other: it was something that would benefit both of us. She concurred.

"Me Against the Music" is still one of my favourite songs, and the collaboration with her is a big part of why.

On the first day of our two or three-day shoot for the song's video, we were told that a seam had come undone on Madonna's white suit and that a seamstress would be coming to mend it, causing a delay in our start time. I ended up having to sit in my trailer for hours while the suit was being repaired.

Really? I pondered. I had no idea taking so much time for myself was an option. I would never make production wait five minutes to fix a broken heel on my shoe. I'd do anything the director said, even if it meant hobbling into the scene without a heel or showing up barefoot. Throughout our session, I was impressed by Madonna's refusal to compromise her vision. She kept the spotlight on herself. Collaboration with Madonna means going along with her ideas and being on her time for days. It was a big lesson for me, one that would take a long time to sink in: she sought authority, and she got it. She was the centre of attention because she made it a need for her to appear anywhere. She carved out that life for herself. I hoped I could do so while retaining the aspects of my nice-girl identity that I wanted to keep.

Chapter 15

In the Zone, my new record, made me joyful. The album's first single, "Me Against the Music," featured Madonna. The following single was "Toxic," for which I received a Grammy Award. "Toxic" was both unique and hugely successful, and it remains one of my favourite songs to perform.

To promote the album, I spent one night in New York City with an MTV camera crew filming a special called In the Zone & Out All Night. We drove all over town to perform at three different nightclubs: Show, Splash, and Avalon. It was thrilling to witness enormous crowds dancing to the new music. My supporters reminded me why I do what I do, as has happened numerous times during my career.

But then there was a knock on my door one day. When I opened the door, four men walked right in, three of whom I didn't recognize. I'd never seen their expressions before.

My father was the fourth.

I invited some friends to my home in Louisiana for the holidays. We were attempting to socialise in the guesthouse I'd built behind the main house, and my mother became irritated with us for being too loud. It suddenly dawned on me that I had enough money to get us out of Louisiana. I planned a vacation to Las Vegas for New Year's Eve, and other of my tourmates joined us.

At the Palms Casino Resort, we let free and drank a lot. I'll admit that we became incredibly foolish. I'll also note that having that much freedom in Sin City was almost overwhelming at times. I was this young girl who had worked so hard, and suddenly the schedule went blank for a few days, so hello, alcohol!

Paris Hilton showed up at the casino to socialise and drink. We were on top of tables, taking our shoes off, and running through the club like fairy-dusted morons before I knew it. No one was wounded, and I had the finest time with Paris—we were just having fun, like we still do whenever we get together.

Nobody was disrespectful to me. It was all in good humour. Most people will undoubtedly judge, and you can't do stuff like that anymore because everyone will pull out their cameras. But back then, in Vegas, we were just being silly. I wasn't interested in generating trouble after having been subjected to so much media scrutiny—it was about feeling free and appreciating what I had worked so hard to acquire.

After a few beers, I ended up in bed with one of my old friends—a childhood pal I'd known my entire life. He and I got shitfaced on the third night we were there together. I don't remember much about that night, but from what I recall, he and I lounged around the hotel room and stayed up late watching movies—Mona Lisa Smile and The Texas Chainsaw Massacre—before deciding to go to A Little White Chapel around three thirty in the morning. We had to wait because another couple was getting married when we arrived. Yes, we had to stand in line to get married.

I've been asked if I love him. To be clear, he and I were not in a relationship. I was simply very drunk—and, in a broader sense at the time in my life, perhaps quite bored.

My entire family flew up to Vegas the next day. They appeared and glared at me with furious eyes. I took a look around. "What happened last night?" I inquired. "Did I kill someone?"

"You got married!" they exclaimed, as if it was somehow worse.

"We were just having some fun," I explained.

But my parents took it very seriously.

"We have to get this annulled," they urged. They made far too much harmless amusement. Everyone has a different view on it, but I didn't take it seriously. A goofy Vegas wedding seems like something people might do as a joke. Then my relatives showed up, acting as if I'd started World War III. I cried for the rest of my trip in Las Vegas.

"I'm guilty!" I exclaimed. "I'm very sorry. "I should not have married."

We signed whatever they asked us to sign. The wedding lasted for 55 hours. I found it odd that they got engaged so soon and decisively—without even giving me a chance to lament what I'd done.

It wasn't that I wanted to establish a family with him or remain with him forever; far from it. And yet, my parents questioned me so much about it that a part of me almost responded, "Hey, maybe I do want to be married!"

Every teenager understands what it's like to desire to rebel against your family, especially if they're abusive. I now realise I was reacting in a very human way. They were placing an unusual amount of pressure on me over something I thought was insignificant—and, in any case, it was my own business.

In fact, my family was so opposed to the wedding that I began to wonder whether I'd done something wonderful by accident. Because I recognized that something about my being under their control and lacking a closer connection to someone else had become really significant to them.

What advantage do I have over you? I was perplexed. Why would someone else pose such a significant threat? It's important to note that by this point, I was financially supporting them.

Everyone was wondering, "Where do you go from here?" And it was an excellent question. I knew the answer. I repeatedly told interviewers that what I really needed was some alone time. I'd begun to fantasise about finding true love and settling down. I felt as if I'd missed out on life.

Chapter 16

We got back on the road. More buses are needed. More racks for costumes. Longer rehearsals. There will be more step-and-repeats.

That was already one of the darkest periods of my life, and the tour's ambiance reflected that—a lot of steamy numbers, gloomy themes, and dreary lighting. My relationship with my brother, Bryan, also changed as a result of the tour.

Bryan, who was now part of my team, was well compensated for the Onyx Hotel Tour, as was I. He also made a big deal with Elizabeth Arden for me. Nonetheless, I found it difficult not to resent him after I embarked on what was to be a really arduous tour while he stayed in Los Angeles and New York and lived his life.

During those years, I lost contact with my brother. As a result, it felt as if I had lost Justin and Bryan at the same time.

I believe that many women, including myself, can be as strong as they want to be, to play this powerful role, but at the end of the day, after we've done our work, made our money, and taken care of everyone else, we want someone to hold us tight and tell us everything will be fine. I apologise. I realise it sounds regressive. But I believe it is a human instinct. We want to feel protected, alive, and sexy all at once. That's exactly what Kevin did for me. So I clutched him like there was no tomorrow.

My friendship with Kevin was initially lighthearted.

Kevin liked me exactly as I was. Being with a man who gave me permission to be exactly who I was seemed like such a gift after spending so much time trying to live up to society's standards.

Even though I was miserable, I had to return to work in the spring of 2004 to meet my contractual obligations. I reasoned that it would be acceptable if Kevin could accompany me, and he agreed to attend. We had so much fun on that tour; he kept me distracted from the work, which felt as difficult as it had ever been. I didn't have to return to my hotel room alone after the shows. We were talking on the plane back home, and I asked him to marry me. He said no, then proposed.

Part of it was because I felt I had earned the right to make my own personal decisions after such a demanding schedule. I felt duped into returning to work immediately after my breakup with Justin since it was all I knew. The Onyx tour was a blunder. But I kept telling myself that I should simply do what I was meant to do, which was work.

I now see that I should have sat back and taken my time getting over Justin's split before resuming touring. The music industry is simply too harsh and cruel. You frequently go to a different city every day. There isn't any consistency. When you're on the road, it's impossible to find peace. When I made Britney Spears: Live and More! video special in Hawaii in 2000, I saw how simple TV can be. Touring is not a luxury in the business; television is.

My sister had also recently secured a lucrative Nickelodeon contract. I was delighted for her. Seeing her practise her lines and do wardrobe fittings made me wish I had a profession that was more like the pleasant world of children's television. I liked recalling the Mickey Mouse Club and how simple everything looked back then.

I expected Kevin to provide me with the stability I desired, as well as the independence I desired.

Many folks were disappointed in Kevin and me. Whether I wanted it or not, I was one of the world's biggest stars at the time. He was leading a more quiet existence. I had to defend our friendship in front of everyone.

That October, Kevin and I married. We had a "surprise" ceremony in September, but the lawyers required extra time to work on the prenup, so the legal event was postponed for a few weeks.

The ceremony was videotaped. The bridesmaids wore burgundy and I wore a strapless gown. After the ceremony, I changed into a pink sweatsuit with the words MRS. FEDERLINE, and everyone else changed into Juicy tracksuits as well, because we were going to a club to dance all night. Now that I was married and contemplating having children, I decided to start saying no to things that didn't feel right, such as the Onyx tour. My bosses and I had a falling out. On my website, I sent a letter to followers in which I announced that I would be taking some time off to enjoy my life.

"I've actually learned to say 'NO!'" I wrote with sincerity. "With this newfound independence, it's as if people aren't sure how to act around me... I apologise for making my life seem chaotic over the last two years. It's most likely because IT WAS! I now understand what they mean when they speak of child stars. Going and going and going has been all I've known since I was fifteen... Please keep in mind that the times are changing, and so am I."

I felt so much better after declaring my determination to finally take control of my own life.

Everything is about to change around here! I thought exuberantly.

Then they did it.

Chapter 17

When I was pregnant, I had two desires: sex and eating. Both of those items were absolutely wonderful with both of my pregnancies.

Aside from that, I can't say there was anything that made me happy. I was simply being cruel. You didn't want to hear from me for two years. I hardly wanted to be around anyone. I was venomous. I didn't want anyone around me, not even my mother. I was a true mother bear. America's sweetheart and the world's meanest woman.

I was also protective of Jamie Lynn. I arrived on the set to confront the actress after she complained to me about a co-star on her TV show. "Are you spreading rumours about my sister?" I must have looked enormously pregnant and ranting at a teenage (and, I later learned, innocent) girl. (I apologise to that young actress.)

When I was pregnant, I told everyone to back off: "Stand back!" There's a baby in the house!

It's true what they say: no one can prepare you for having a baby. It's nothing short of miraculous. You're constructing a new body. You grow up saying, "That person's pregnant." "That person had a baby." But when you actually go through it, it's overwhelming. It was a spiritual experience, with an immensely strong link.

My mother had often mentioned how terrible childbirth could be. She never let me forget that she'd been in terrible labour with me for many hours. Everyone is unique, after all. Some ladies have it easier than others. I was frightened about having a natural birth. I was overjoyed when the doctor suggested a C-section.

On September 14, 2005, Sean Preston was born. You could tell he was a sweet, caring little boy right away.

Three months later, I became pregnant again. I was overjoyed to have two kids so close in age. Still, it was difficult for my body, and I felt a lot of sadness and loneliness at the time. I felt like the entire universe was conspiring against me.

The primary hazard I had to watch out for was paparazzi assault.

If I stayed out of the spotlight, the cameras would definitely leave me alone, I reasoned. Photographers tracked me down whether I was at home or attempting to go to the store. They were there every day and night, waiting for me to come out.

Nobody in the media appeared to notice that I was already harsh on myself. I might be crazy, but I was always a people-pleaser at heart. Even when I was at my lowest, I cared what other people thought of me. I grew up in the South, where manners are highly valued. To this day, regardless of their age, I address men as "sir" and ladies as "ma'am." Just on the level of etiquette, it was excruciating to be treated with such contempt—with loathing.

I documented everything I did with the babies. When I drove away from the paparazzi with Sean Preston on my lap, it was interpreted as proof that I was unfit. I was cornered by paparazzi with him at the Malibu Country Mart as well—they kept taking my picture while I held him and cried.

I was surrounded by photographers as I attempted to exit a building and into a car in New York, pregnant with Jayden James and carrying Sean Preston. I was told I had to enter the car on the other side, so I said, "Oh," and made my way through a thousand camera shutters and yells of "Britney! Britney!" to get in.

If you watch the movie rather than just the still photographs, you'll notice that while carrying a cup of water in one hand and my kid in the other, my heel rotated and I almost fell—but I didn't. And in catching myself, I didn't drop the water or the baby, who, by the way, was unfazed.

"This is why I need a gun," I told the camera, which probably didn't go down well. But I was at a loss for words. The mags seemed to want nothing more than a shot with the title "Britney Spears got HUGE!" She's not even wearing makeup!" As if those two things were a sin—as if gaining weight was something cruel I'd done to them, a betrayal. When did I decide to stay seventeen for the rest of my life?

Chapter 18

Jayden James was born on September 12, 2006, just before Sean Preston's first birthday. From the moment he was born, he was a cheerful child.

I felt so light after I'd had both sons, almost like I was a bird or a feather, like I could glide away.

My body felt amazing to me. Is this what being a thirteen-year-old feels like again? I pondered. I no longer had a stomach.

"Wow, you look so skinny!" exclaimed one of my pals.

"Well, I've been pregnant for two years straight," she replied.

I felt like an entirely different person after the babies. It was perplexing.

On the one hand, I found myself unexpectedly fitting back into my clothes. When I tried them on, they looked great! It was a revelation to rediscover my love for clothes. I said, "Holy sh*t!" My entire body!

On the other hand, I'd been so relieved to know that these babies were safe inside of me. When I couldn't keep them secure inside my body anymore, I became depressed. They appeared so defenceless in the world of squabbling paparazzi and tabloids. I wanted them back inside me, away from the rest of the world.

One headline asked, "Why is Britney so camera-shy with Jayden?"

After Jayden was born, Kevin and I had gotten so good at hiding the kids that many were puzzled why no images of him had been released. I believe that if anyone had given the question a second consideration, they could have made some educated guesses. However, no one was actually asking the question. They just continued acting as if I owed it to them to let the men who were always attempting to catch me looking fat snap pictures of my infant sons.

One of the first things I had to do after each birth was count the number of enemy combatants in the parking lot. Every time I checked, they seemed to multiply. There were constantly more cars than appeared to be safe. Seeing so many men gathered to photograph my children made my blood run cold. With a lot of money on the line in photo rights, it was their duty to capture images of the guys at any cost.

And my boys were so small. It was my responsibility to keep them secure. I was concerned that the flashing lights and shouts would startle them. Kevin and I had to create techniques to cover them with blankets while still allowing them to breathe. I couldn't even do it without a blanket.

I wasn't interested in conducting publicity that year, although I did do one interview for Dateline with Matt Lauer. People were asking him about me, he added, including "Is Britney a bad mom?" He never stated who was questioning them. Everyone, it appears. And he inquired as to what I believed it would take for the paparazzi to leave me alone. I wished he'd asked them so that whatever it was, I could do it.

Fortunately, my house was a secure haven. Our marriage was in turmoil, but Kevin and I had constructed an amazing mansion in Los Angeles, right next door to Mel Gibson's. Sandy from Grease also lived close. When I saw her, I'd say, "Hi, Olivia Newton-John! Olivia Newton-John, how are you?"

It was a dream home for us. The pool was accessible by a slide. There was a sandbox with toys for the youngsters to build sandcastles in. We had a tiny playhouse with steps and a ladder, as well as a tiny porch. And we just kept building on it.

I didn't like the wooden floors, so I replaced them with marble—of course, white marble.

The interior designer was adamantly opposed. He went on to say, "Marble floors are super slippery and hard if you fall down."

"I want marble!" I yelled. "I need marble."

It was both my house and my nest. It was just stunning. But I guess I realised then that I'd turned strange.

I'd had these two children consecutively. My hormones were out of control. I was cruel as heck and extremely dictatorial. Having children was a huge thing for me. I had gone beyond in my efforts to make our home perfect. Now that I think about it, that was terrible. Please accept my apologies, contractors. I believe I was overly concerned.

I hired a muralist to create imaginative images of small boys on the moon for the boys' rooms. I simply went all out.

It had always been my desire to have children and raise them in the most comfortable setting I could devise. They were wonderful, lovely, and everything I'd ever desired. I wanted to give them the entire solar system.

When I refused to let my mother hold Jayden for the first two months, I began to suspect that I was being overprotective. Even after that, I'd only let her hold him for five minutes. I needed him back in my arms. That is excessive. That I now understand. I should not have been so commanding.

Again, I believe what happened when I first saw them after they were born was similar to what happened to me after Justin's breakup: it was the Benjamin Button effect. I went back in time. As a new mother, I felt as if a piece of me had become a baby. One part of me was a demanding adult shrieking about white marble, while another part of me became quite childlike.

In some ways, children are extremely healing. They make you less critical. Here they are, helpless and reliant on you. You realise that everyone was once a baby, frail and defenceless. In another aspect, having children was a mentally difficult experience for me. It had happened before Jamie Lynn was born. I loved her so much and was so sympathetic that I somehow became her. When she turned three, a part of me turned three as well.

I've heard that this may happen to parents, especially if you have childhood trauma. When your children reach the age you were when you were dealing with a difficult situation, you emotionally relive it.

Unfortunately, there was no such discussion about mental health back then as there is now. I hope that any new mothers reading this who are struggling would seek help as soon as possible and channel their emotions into something more soothing than white marble floors. Because I now know that I was experiencing almost every perinatal depression symptom: sorrow, anxiety, and exhaustion. When the infants were delivered, I contributed to my perplexity and anxiety with the babies' safety, which was intensifying as more media attention was focused on us. Being a new mother is difficult enough without having to do everything under the microscope.

With Kevin absent so frequently, no one was present to see my spiral—except every paparazzi in America.

Chapter 19

Those first few months after Jayden returned home flew by. I bought a dog. Felicia came and went in and out of my life.

I liked that no one was overthinking things and that I was able to express what I liked and disliked. I understood exactly what I wanted, and I loved a lot of what was presented to me. It was exciting to get into the studio and hear these beautiful sounds and then record a vocal over them. Despite my reputation at the time, I arrived determined and eager to work. What was going on outside the studio was the most upsetting.

The paparazzi were like a zombie army, attempting to get in at every opportunity. They attempted to scale the walls and snap photographs through the windows. Attempting to enter and depart a building felt like a military operation. It was frightening.

Teresa LaBarbera Whites, my A&R rep who was also a mother, did everything she could to assist. She installed a baby swing in one of our studios, which I thought was a very thoughtful gift.

The album served as a sort of rallying call. After years of being precise in order to impress my mother and father, it was time to say "Fuck you." I stopped doing business the way I had always done it. I began filming footage on the street alone. I'd go into pubs with a friend who'd just bring a camera, and that's how we shot "Gimme More."

To be clear, I'm not bragging about it. "Gimme More" is by far the worst video I've ever created. I despise it because it is so tacky. It appears that we spent only three thousand dollars to shoot it. Nonetheless, despite its flaws, it served its purpose. And the more I went and did things for myself, the more intriguing people began to notice and want to work with me. By word of mouth, I ended up meeting some pretty nice folks at random.

Blackout was one of the simplest and most rewarding albums I've ever made. It came together quite quickly. I'd walk into the studio, stay for thirty minutes, and then go. That wasn't on purpose; it had to be quick. If I stayed in one spot for too long, the photographers outside would multiply like Pac-Man being pursued by ghosts. My survival strategy was to get in and out of studios as quickly as possible.

When I went into the studio to record "Hot as Ice," there were six huge guys sitting there with me. Being with all those gentlemen quietly listening to me sing was perhaps one of the most spiritual recording experiences of my life. My voice rose to its greatest pitch. I sang it again and then departed. I didn't have to even attempt.

Even though making Blackout felt amazing, life was still staring at me from all sides. Everything was so severe from one minute to the next. I needed more self-worth and value than I could muster at the time. Even though it was a difficult time in almost every other way, it was fantastic artistically. Something about my mental state made me a better artist.

Making the Blackout record gave me a rush. I had the opportunity to work in the best studios. It was an exciting time.

Unfortunately, when family life is poor, it takes over and makes everything else feel better. I lament how bad things got with my family, but I'm still quite proud of that CD. Many musicians have stated that it affected them, and many fans have stated that it is their favourite.

Meanwhile, Kevin was getting a lot of coverage, as if he'd just hit a grand slam in the World Series. I had forgotten who he was. Then he was approached to appear in a Nationwide Super Bowl commercial. It didn't matter that the ad featured him making fun of himself as a fast-food worker who aspires to be a celebrity. I never saw him again after he accepted that deal. It was as if he was too good to talk to me. He told everyone that becoming a father meant everything to him, that it was the best thing in his life. You'd never guess. Because, unfortunately, he was away a lot.

Chapter 20

When I married Kevin, I did it wholeheartedly. Look into my eyes in my wedding photos to realise how much I was in love and ready for a new chapter in my life to begin. I wanted children with this man. I desired a comfortable home. I wished to grow old alongside him.

Kevin, according to my lawyer, would file for divorce if I did not. I deduced from this that Kevin wanted to file for divorce but felt horrible about it. He understood that if I filed, it would make him appear better in public. Kevin, according to my lawyer, was going to file for divorce regardless. I was made to believe that doing it first would save me from embarrassment.

I didn't want to be ashamed, so I submitted the papers in early November 2006, when Jayden was almost two months old. Kevin and I both requested exclusive custody of the boys. What I didn't realise was that Kevin would then demand that I pay for his legal fees. And because I had formally initiated the divorce, I would be held accountable in the public for breaking up my young family.

The media coverage was insane. It was probably excellent for Kevin's CD, which was released a week before we announced our divorce, but I got slammed. Some individuals tried to be supportive, but in the press, they frequently did so by being harsh to Kevin, which wasn't very helpful.

I gave a speech at the American Music Awards later that month. While I was waiting to go onstage, Jimmy Kimmel performed a monologue and a spoof about Kevin, whom he referred to as "the world's first-ever no-hit wonder." They put a stand-in in a crate, loaded it onto a truck, and dumped it in the water.

This, however, was the father of my two infant sons. I was disturbed by the violence directed at him. The entire audience burst out laughing. I had no idea it was going to happen, and it really threw me off guard. I went on onstage and presented the award to Mary J. Blige, but then I returned backstage and attempted to make it apparent that I had been taken aback and didn't enjoy it. I also didn't think that having my ex-husband treated that way would help me in the midst of a custody battle.

Everyone appeared pleased with the news of our divorce—everyone but me. I had no desire to celebrate.

In retrospect, I believe Justin and Kevin were both very astute. They knew what they were doing, and I was right there with them.

That's the thing with this business. I had no idea how to play the game. On whatever level, I had no idea how to express myself. I used to be a lousy dresser, and I'll admit that I still am. And I'm working on it. I will try. But, as much as I will admit my weaknesses, I know that I am a nice guy. I can see now that you had to be smart, ruthless, and deliberate to play the game, and I didn't know what the game was. I was really innocent—just oblivious. I was a recently single mother of two small boys, and I didn't have time to straighten my hair before entering a sea of photographers.

So I was young and made many blunders. But I will say this: I was not deceptive. I was simply stupid.

Justin and Kevin wrecked one aspect of my personality. I used to have faith in people. But after my divorce and my separation with Justin, I never trusted anyone again.

Chapter 21

Paris Hilton was one of the sweetest individuals to me when I really needed it. Much of America rejected her as a party girl, but I thought she was elegant—the way she stood on the red carpet and always had an arched eyebrow when someone said something negative about her.

She noticed that I had babies and was going through a breakup, and I believe she felt sorry for me. She came over to my house and was quite helpful. She was quite sweet to me. Aside from that night in Vegas with Jason Trawick, no one had been so lovely to me in a long time. We began to hang out. For the first time in a long time, she urged me to attempt to have fun.

I went through my party stage with Paris. But, to be clear, it was never as wild as the media made it out to be. I used to spend hardly any time outside. Finally, when I left home for a few hours with the kids properly supervised at home by qualified caregivers, remained out late, and drank like any other twentysomething, I heard nothing but that I was the worst mother who'd ever lived and a terrible person. The headlines were rife with accusations: She's a slacker! She's high on drugs!

I never had an alcohol issue. I enjoyed drinking, but it was never out of hand. Do you want to know what my go-to medicine is? Apart from drinking, what else did I do? Adderall is an amphetamine that is prescribed to children for ADHD. Yes, Adderall got me high, but what I found far more enticing was that it made me feel less depressed for a few hours. It was the only drug that worked for me as an antidepressant, and I desperately needed one.

I've never been interested in hard drugs. I saw lots of musicians performing all of that, but it wasn't for me. Where I grew up, we drank beer more than anything else; to this day, I avoid drinking costly wine because it hurts my throat. And, other than that one time in New York when I injured my heel, I've never enjoyed cannabis. It makes me feel stupid and foolish if I only get a high contact from being around it. It irritates me.

Do you know what Paris and I did on that purportedly insane night with Lindsay Lohan that everyone made such a big deal about? We got wasted. That's all!

I walked inside the beach house at the end of one night, satisfied with my excursion but still a touch tipsy.

My mother was waiting for me. She screamed at me when I stepped in, and we got into a huge fight.

She said it was due to my inebriation.

My heart was killed by the embarrassment I felt. Okay, I thought as I stood there reeling. I guess it's illegal for me to party.

My mother was continually making me feel awful or guilty of something, even though I had worked so hard to be decent. That's how my family has always treated me: as if I were bad. The fight was a watershed moment in my relationship with my mother. I couldn't go back to how things were before. We tried, but it didn't work out.

My parents never appeared to think I was worth anything, no matter how many followers I had throughout the world. How could you treat your child this way while she was going through a divorce, lonely and lost?

Giving someone no grace during a difficult moment is simply not nice, especially when you can't take as well as you give. They didn't like it when I started to speak up and throw it back at them a little— God knows they weren't perfect. But they still had a strong emotional hold on me.

Chapter 22

For me, everything everyone says about being a mom was true. My boys give meaning to my life. I was quite aback by how much genuine and immediate affection I felt for those small beings.

However, being a mother while under so much pressure at home and in the world was far more difficult than I had anticipated.

I began to act strange after being cut off from my buddies. I know you're meant to focus solely on being a mother during those times, but it was difficult for me to sit down and play with them every day, to prioritise being a mother. I was completely perplexed. Everything I'd known my entire life was being revealed on every level. I had no idea where to go or what to do. Was I supposed to go home to Louisiana, build a wall around my house, and hide?

Kevin attempted to persuade everyone that I was utterly out of control as part of his effort for full custody. He began to suggest that I should not have my children at all.

When he stated that, I thought to myself, "Surely this is a joke." This is strictly for the tabloids. When you hear about married celebrities quarrelling, you never know what's true. I usually assume that a lot of what you hear is a ruse to obtain the upper hand in a custody dispute by feeding things to the papers. So I waited for him to return the boys to me once he had taken them. He not only refused to return them to me, but he also refused to allow me to see them for weeks on end.

Sandra, my aunt, died in January 2007 after a long and arduous battle with ovarian cancer. She was like a second mother to me. At the burial, I cried harder than I ever had before over Aunt Sandra's grave.

I declined because I believed it would be detrimental to my emotional health. But I wonder if simply knowing the part made me instinctively go there in my thoughts and envision what it would be like to be her.

I'd been feeling a veil of darkness on the inside for a long time. On the outside, though, I'd attempted to keep looking and acting the way others expected me to—sweet and attractive all the time. But the sheen had worn away to the point that there was nothing left. I was like a raw nerve.

I went to beg to see the boys in February, after not seeing them for weeks and weeks, absolutely overcome with grief. Kevin refused to let me in. I pleaded with him. Sean Preston was seventeen months old and Jayden James was five months old. I pictured them wondering why their mother didn't want to be with them because they didn't know where she was. I intended to attack them with a battering ram. I had no idea what to do.

The paparazzi were present throughout. I can't put into words how humiliated I felt. I was surrounded. I was out and about, being pursued by these men who were waiting for me to do anything they could photograph.

So I provided them with some material that night.

I went to a hair salon and shaved off all of my hair with clippers.

It was hilarious to everyone. Look how insane she is! My parents were also humiliated by me. Nobody seemed to grasp that I was just insane with grief. My children had been abducted from me.

Everyone, including my mother, was terrified of me with my head shaved. No one would talk to me because I was too unattractive.

I was aware that my long hair was a large part of what people appreciated about me. I was aware that many men believed long hair was attractive.

Shaving my head was my way of telling the world, "Fuck you!" You want me to look nice for you? You're a jerk. You expect me to be good to you? You're a jerk. Do you want me to be your fantasy girl? You're a jerk. For years, I'd been a good girl. I'd smiled politely as TV show hosts mocked my breasts, while American parents said I was destroying their children by wearing a crop top, while executives patted my hand condescendingly and questioned my career choices despite selling millions of records, and while my family acted like I was evil. And I was fed up with it.

I didn't care at the end of the day. All I wanted was to see my boys. It made me sick to think about the hours, days, and weeks I spent away from them. My favourite memories are of taking naps with my children. Taking naps with my lovely infants, smelling their hair, holding their little hands—that's the closest I've ever felt to God.

I grew quite enraged. I believe many other ladies feel the same way. "If someone took my baby away from me, I would have done a lot more than get a haircut," a buddy of mine once commented. "I would have set fire to the city."

Chapter 23

I lost it over and over again over those weeks without my children. I didn't even know how to look after myself. I'd had to leave the house I loved due to the divorce and was now living in a strange English-style cottage in Beverly Hills. The paparazzi were buzzing around like sharks when there's blood in the sea.

It seemed almost sacred when I initially shaved my head. I was living on a pure being level.

For when I needed to go out into the world, I ordered seven short bob wigs. But I didn't want to see anyone if I couldn't see my sons.

My cousin Alli drove me back to Kevin's a few days after I shaved my head. At the very least, I expected no paparazzi to be present this time. However, one of the photographers was reportedly tipped off, and he contacted his pal.

They came looking for me when we stopped at a gas station. They kept snapping flash photos with a large camera and videotaping me through the window while I sat in the passenger seat, devastated, waiting for Alli to return. "How are you doing?," one of them inquired. How are you doing? "I'm worried about you."

We continued on to Kevin's. The two paparazzi continued to follow us, capturing pictures as I was denied admittance to Kevin's once more. I turned away, hoping to get a glimpse of my own children.

Alli pulled over after we departed so we could figure out what to do next. The videographer had returned to my window.

"What I'm going to do, Britney—all I'm going to do—is ask you a few questions," one of them remarked, a cruel expression on his face. He didn't ask if he could. He was preparing to do something for me. "And then I'm going to leave you alone."

Alli began pleading with the men to leave her alone. "Please, gentlemen. Guys, don't do it. "Please, please..."

She was so courteous, and she was appealing with them as if she was begging them to save our lives, which she was.

But they wouldn't give up. I yelled.

They liked it when I reacted. One man refused to go until he got his way. He kept smirking and asking me the same horrible questions over and over, hoping I'd react again. His voice was filled with harshness and a lack of humanity.

This was one of the darkest times in my life, and he pursued me. Couldn't he just treat me like a human? Could he not back down? But he refused. He simply kept coming. He kept asking me how I felt about not being able to see my children. He was beaming.

I finally snapped.

I jumped out of the car with the only thing I could reach, a green umbrella. I wasn't going to punch him because, even in my worst moments, I'm not that type of guy. I smashed into the next nearest item, which happened to be his automobile.

Really, it's pathetic. A raincoat. You can't even hurt yourself with an umbrella. A desperate person made a desperate move.

I was so embarrassed by what I'd done that I wrote an apology email to the photo agency, noting that I'd been considered for a dark film role, which was true, and that I wasn't quite myself, which was also true.

Later, in an interview for a documentary about me, that paparazzo would observe, "That was not a good night for her... But it was a terrific night for us since we got the game-winning shot."

My husband, Hesam, now informs me that shaved heads are a thing for beautiful girls. It's a mood, he adds, a decision not to conform to conventional beauty standards. He tries to help me feel better about it because he is saddened by how much it still bothers me.

Chapter 24

I felt as if I were living on the precipice of a cliff.

I went to Bryan's residence in Los Angeles after shaving my head. He was accompanied by two women from his past in Mississippi, as well as my mother. My mother didn't even look at me since I was so unattractive. It just demonstrated that the world is primarily concerned about your physical look, even if you are in pain and at your lowest point.

I'd been informed that going to rehab would help me regain custody that winter. So, despite the fact that I believed I had a fury and grief problem rather than a substance misuse problem, I went. My father was present when I arrived. He sat across from me, with three picnic tables in between. He told her, "You are a disgrace."

When I reflect back, I wonder why I didn't call Big Rob for assistance. I was already ashamed and embarrassed, and now my father was calling me a disgrace. It was the epitome of flogging a dead horse. He was treating me like a dog, a very nasty dog. I had no one. I felt completely alone. One advantage of rehab was that I began the healing process. I was adamant about making the best of a bad circumstance.

When I was released, I was able to obtain interim joint custody through the assistance of an excellent attorney. But the battle with Kevin raged on, and it was eating me alive.

Blackout, the project I'm most pleased of in my entire career, was released right around Halloween in 2007. I was supposed to perform "Gimme More" at the Video Music Awards to help promote it. I didn't want to, but my team was putting pressure on me to go out there and prove to the world that I was fine.

The only difficulty with this strategy was that I wasn't feeling well.

Nothing was going right backstage at the VMAs that night. My costume and hair extensions were both malfunctioning. I hadn't gotten any sleep the night before. I felt woozy. It had been less than a year since I'd delivered my second child in two years, yet everyone was making fun of my lack of six-pack abs. I couldn't believe I had to go up onstage feeling the way I did.

Backstage, I ran into Justin. I hadn't seen him in a long time. Everything was going swimmingly in his world. He was at the top of his game in every manner, and he exuded confidence. I was experiencing a panic attack. I hadn't practised enough. I despised the way I looked. I could tell it was going to be horrible.

I went out there and did my best at the time, which was, admittedly, far from my best at other times. While performing, I could see myself on camera throughout the auditorium; it was like staring in a fun-house mirror.

I'm not going to justify or say that the performance was wonderful, but as performers, we all have bad nights. They don't normally have such severe repercussions.

The newspapers mocked my body and my performance in the days and weeks that followed. Dr. Phil described it as a train wreck.

When Blackout was released in October 2007, the only press I did was a live radio interview with Ryan Seacrest. During the interview, Ryan Seacrest asked me questions such as, "How do you respond to those who criticise you as a mom?" with the question "Do you feel like you're doing everything you can for your kids?" with the question "How often will you see them?"

It seemed like that was all everybody wanted to speak about: whether or not I was a fit mother. Not about how I'd created such a powerful record while carrying two babies on my hips and being pursued by dozens of dangerous men every day.

My management team resigned. As a witness in the custody dispute, a bodyguard appeared in court with Gloria Allred by his side. He said I was using narcotics, but he was not cross-examined.

A parenting coach assigned by the court stated that I adored my children and that we were definitely attached. She also stated that there was nothing in my home that could be classified as abuse.

But that didn't make the news.

Chapter 25

I had the boys one day in early January 2008, and at the end of the visit, a security guard who used to work for me but now worked for Kevin arrived to bring them up.

First, he loaded Preston into the car. When he arrived to pick up Jayden, I realised I might never see my boys again. Given the state of my custody case, I was frightened that if I returned the children, I wouldn't see them again.

I dashed into the bathroom with Jayden and locked the door—I couldn't bear the thought of him leaving. I didn't want anyone to take my child. A friend arrived at the bathroom door and informed me that the security guy would wait. I sobbed as I held Jayden. But no one was willing to give me more time. Before I knew it, a SWAT team in black suits pushed through the restroom door, as if I'd done something wrong. The only thing I was guilty of was being anxious to keep my own children for a few more hours and to receive some assurance that I wouldn't lose them permanently. I just glanced at my pal and said, "But you said he'd wait..."

After they had Jayden, they handcuffed me to a gurney and drove me to the hospital.

The hospital released me before the 72-hour hold was up. However, the harm had already been done. It didn't help that the paparazzi were becoming more aggressive in their pursuit of me.

A fresh custody court was convened, and I was told that because I'd panicked because I was afraid of losing the kids, I'd be permitted to see them even less.

Nobody seemed to have my back. Even my relatives appeared unconcerned. I learned of my sixteen-year-old sister's pregnancy from a tabloid exclusive over the holidays. It had been hidden from me by my family. This was around the time Jamie Lynn was on the verge of filing for emancipation from our parents. Taking away her cell phone is one of the things she has accused them of. She was forced to communicate with the outside world using burner phones that she kept hidden.

I now understand that if someone isn't doing well—and I wasn't doing well—that's the moment to come to that person and hold them. Kevin took away my entire universe. He sucked the life out of me. And neither did my relatives.

I began to suspect that they were secretly applauding the fact that I was going through the worst period of my life. But that couldn't be right, could it? Surely, I was insane.

Right?

Chapter 26

All year, Los Angeles is warm and sunny. Driving across the city, it can be difficult to recall what season it is. People are wearing sunglasses and drinking cool drinks through straws everywhere you turn, smiling and laughing beneath the clear blue sky. But in January 2008, even in California, it seemed like winter because I was alone and freezing, and I was hospitalised.

I probably shouldn't confess it, but I was a wreck. I was on a high dose of Adderall.

I was terrible, and I will acknowledge that I made mistakes. I was furious at what had happened to Kevin. I'd tried everything with him. I'd given everything I had.

And he'd turned against me.

I'd begun dating a photographer. I was completely smitten by him. He'd been a paparazzo, and I knew many suspected him of wrongdoing, but all I could see at the time was that he was gallant and helped me out when the others became too pushy.

I had no dread.

I had no idea the photographer was married; I had no idea I was effectively his mistress. I only found out after we'd split up. I'd just thought he was a lot of fun, and our time together had been quite heated. He was ten years my senior.

The photographers were wherever I went—and I went out a lot for a spell. Despite all of the claims about my being out of control, I don't believe I was ever out of control in a way that justified what happened next. The reality is that I was quite sad and missed my children while they were with Kevin.

The photographer assisted me in overcoming my sadness. I yearned for attention, and he provided it to me. It was purely a sexual relationship. My family didn't like him, but I didn't like a lot of things about them.

I was encouraged to rebel by the photographer. He still loved me even though he let me sow my oats. He loved me completely. It wasn't like my mother was yelling at me for going out. He went on to say, "Girl, go, you got it, do your thing!" He wasn't like my father, who made enormous demands on his affection.

So, with the photographer's help, I did my thing completely. And being that daring seemed radical. That was far from what everyone expected of me.

I was speaking as if I were insane. I was obnoxious everywhere I went, including restaurants. People would take me out to lunch, and I would lie down on the table. It was my way of shouting "Fuck you!" to anybody who crossed my path.

I mean, I'll own it: I was bad.

Or perhaps I wasn't so much evil as angry.

I wished to flee. I didn't have any children, and I needed to stay away from the press and photographers. I needed to get out of LA, so the photographer and I took a trip to Mexico.

It was as if I'd escaped to a secure haven. Outside my door, there would be a million people everywhere else. But even though I was only gone for a brief period, I felt disconnected from everything. This helped; I felt better for a short time. I should have taken use of it more.

My relationship with the photographer appeared to be becoming more serious, and as this occurred, I sensed that my family was trying to draw closer to me—in an unsettling way.

"Britney, we feel like something's going on," my mother stated one day. We've heard the cops are after you. "Let's go to the beach."

"The cops are after me?" I inquired. "For what?" I'd done nothing illegal. That I was certain of. I'd had my ups and downs. I'd had my wild phase. I'd been high on Adderall and had been acting nuts. But I didn't commit any crimes. In fact, as she was aware, I'd spent the previous two days with women. My mother and I had spent the night with my cousin Alli and two other women.

I eventually realised that something had changed from the last time I was taken to the hospital for assessment that month. My father had developed a close bond with Louise "Lou" Taylor, whom he idolised. She was at the forefront of the conservatorship's implementation, which would eventually let them manage and take over my career. Lou, who had recently founded a new company called Tri Star Sports & Entertainment Group, was intimately involved in making decisions prior to the conservatorship. She had few genuine clients at the time. She practically built her company on my name and hard work.

Conservatorships, also known as guardianships, are often reserved for those who lack mental capacity and are unable to make decisions for themselves. But I was quite functional. I'd just completed my best album to date. I was producing a lot of money for a lot of people, including my father, who I later discovered took a higher income than he paid me. He paid himself over $6 million, while those connected to him received tens of millions more.

The point is, you can have a conservatorship for two months and then let the person get their life back on track, but that wasn't what my father intended. He desired far more.

My father was able to establish two types of conservatorship: "conservatorship of the person" and "conservatorship of the estate."

The conservator of the individual is in charge of the conservatee's daily life, including where they reside, what they eat, whether they can drive a car, and what they do. Even though I asked the court to appoint anyone else—and I mean, anyone off the street would have been better—my father was appointed, the same man who used to make me cry when I was a little girl because he talked to himself. And I was informed in court that I was insane, and I wasn't even permitted to choose my own lawyer.

The conservator of the estate—in my instance, an estate worth tens of millions of dollars at one point—manages the affairs of the conservatee to keep them from being "subject to undue influence or fraud." My father took on this position in collaboration with a lawyer named Andrew Wallet, who would eventually be paid $426,000 per year to block me from my own money. I'd be obliged to pay my court-appointed lawyer, whom I couldn't replace, upwards of $500,000 every year.

My father and Lou's staff Robin Greenhill seemed to dominate my life and watch every move I made. I'm a 5-foot-4-inch pop singer who addresses everyone as "sir" and "ma'am." They acted as if I were a criminal or a predator.

There were times when I needed my father and sought out him, but he wasn't there. But when it came time for him to be the conservator, he was there! He's always been obsessed with money.

I can't claim my mother was any better. She'd pretended to be innocent throughout her two overnight nights with my girlfriends and myself. She'd known they were going to take me away the whole time. I'm confident it was all premeditated, and that my father, mother, and Lou Taylor were all involved. Tri Star was even considering becoming my co-conservator. Later, I discovered that at the time they placed me in conservatorship, on the heels of his bankruptcy, my father was financially indebted to Lou, owing her at least $40,000, which was a large sum for him at the time. That was later referred to in court as a "conflict of interest" by my new counsel, Mathew Rosengart.

I was informed shortly after being taken to the hospital against my will that conservatorship paperwork had been filed.

Chapter 27

The conservatorship was allegedly established because I was unable to do anything—feeding myself, spending my own money, being a mother, anything. So why would they have me shoot an episode of How I Met Your Mother a few weeks later and then send me on a tough global tour?

My mother and my brother's girlfriend got short haircuts and went out to dinner drinking wine after the conservatorship began— paparazzi were there shooting their pictures. It all felt pre-planned. My father had taken away my boyfriend, and I was unable to drive. My mother and father stripped me of my womanhood. It was a win-win situation for them.

I was still astounded that the state of California would let a man like my father—an alcoholic, someone who'd declared bankruptcy, failed in business, and had terrified me as a child—control me after all my accomplishments and everything I'd done.

I reflected on the counsel my father had given me throughout the years that I had ignored, and I worried if I would be able to do so again. My father pitched the conservatorship as a significant step in my "comeback." I'd just released the best record of my career a few months before, but that was alright. What I heard my father say was, "She's great now!" She works for us! It's a fantastic opportunity for our family."

Was it beneficial to me? Or was it fantastic for him?

What a blast! I pondered. I can go back to work as if nothing had occurred! Too sick to pick my own boyfriend, but still healthy enough to appear on sitcoms and morning shows and perform for thousands of people in different parts of the world every week!

From that moment on, I began to believe that he considered me as being put on the planet solely to enhance their financial flow.

At my residence, my father converted my small study and bar area into his office. There was a bowl with a bunch of receipts in it.

Yes, I will admit it: I was such a nerd that I saved all of my receipts in a bowl. To keep track of my tax deductions, I would total up my costs each week the old-fashioned way. Even when I was going through a hard patch, the foundations of who I was as a person remained. That bowl of receipts proved to me that I could still manage my affairs. I know musicians who smoked heroin, got into fights, and hurled televisions out hotel windows. Not only did I not steal, harm anyone, or use strong drugs, but I was also keeping track of my tax deductions.

Not any longer. My father pushed my receipt dish aside and arranged his belongings on the bar. "I just wanted to let you know," he added, "that I make the decisions." You sit in that chair, and I'll tell you what's going on."

I was becoming increasingly terrified as I looked at him.

"I'm Britney Spears now," he explained.

Chapter 28

On the rare occasions when I went out, such as to my agent and friend Cade's house for a dinner party, the security team would go through the house before I arrived to ensure there was no alcohol, drugs, or even Tylenol. No one at the gathering was permitted to consume alcohol until I left. The other attendees were all great sports about it, but I had a feeling that the actual party began the moment I departed.

I promptly contacted the strange-as-hell lawyer the court had selected for me and requested for his assistance. Despite the fact that I hadn't selected him, he was all I really had. I was advised that I couldn't hire somebody new since my lawyer had to be approved by the court. Much later, I would discover it was nonsense: I had no idea for thirteen years that I could have hired my own lawyer. I had the impression that the court-appointed lawyer was uninterested in assisting me in understanding what was going on or in fighting for my rights.

My mother, who is best friends with Louisiana's governor, could have called him and he would have told me I could hire my own lawyer. But mom kept it a secret; instead, she hired a lawyer for herself so she could continue battling with my father, as she had done when I was younger.

I resisted several times, especially when my father took away my cell phone. I'd smuggle in a private phone and try to escape. But they were continuously catching me.

And here's the terrible, honest truth: I didn't have much fight left in me after everything I'd been through. I was exhausted and terrified. After being restrained on a gurney, I was aware that they may confine my body at any time. They may have tried to kill me, I reasoned. I began to worry if they truly intended to murder me.

When my father said, "I call the shots," I thought to myself, "This is too much for me." But I couldn't see an escape. So I felt my spirit withdraw and went into autopilot mode. If I play along, they'll probably see how good I am and let me leave.

As a result, I agreed to it.

It's difficult for me to revisit this worst period of my life and consider what may have been different if I'd fought harder back then. That is something I despise even thinking about. To be honest, I can't afford it. I've been through a lot.

And it was true that I had been partying when the conservatorship occurred. That was too much for my body to bear. It was time to relax. But I went from being a big partier to a total hermit. I did nothing during the conservatorship.

I was reunited with my boys because I followed the rules.

It was a thrilling pleasure to be able to hold them again. For the first time in months, I felt complete as they fell asleep next to me on the first night we were back together. I just glanced at them sleeping and felt incredibly fortunate.

I tried everything I could to placate Kevin so that I could see them as frequently as possible. I paid his legal bills, child support, and hundreds of dollars more each month so the kids could accompany me on the Circus Tour. I appeared on Good Morning America, did the Los Angeles Christmas tree lighting, shot an Ellen feature, and toured Europe and Australia all in the same week. But the question persisted: if I was so sick that I couldn't make my own decisions, why did they believe it was okay for me to be out there smiling, waving, singing, and dancing in a million time zones every week?

Let me give you one good reason.

The Circus Tour grossed about $130 million dollars.

Tri Star, Lou Taylor's company, received 5%. After the conservatorship, I discovered that even though I was on leave in 2019 and no money was coming in, my father gave them an extra minimum "flat fee," meaning they were paid hundreds of thousands of dollars more.

My father received a share as well, as well as roughly $16,000 each month throughout the conservatorship, which was more than he'd ever made before. He became a multimillionaire as a result of the conservatorship.

I was willing to give up my independence in return for naps with my children. Nothing makes me happier or more significant on this planet than my children. I'd give my life for them.

So, I reasoned, why not my liberty?

Chapter 29

How do you hold on to hope? I had resolved to comply with the conservatorship for the sake of my sons, but being a part of it was really difficult. I knew there was something more inside of me, but it was diminishing by the day. The fire within me died out over time. My eyes lost their light. I know my admirers saw it, even if they didn't really comprehend what had occurred because I was so tightly controlled.

I feel a lot of sympathy for the woman I was before being placed in the conservatory, while I was recording Blackout. Despite being described as a wayward and wild girl, all of my best work was completed during that period. Overall, however, it was a miserable period. I had two small children, and every time I tried to see them, there was a conflict.

Looking back, I believe that if I had been wise, I would have done nothing but focus on my life at home, no matter how difficult it was.

Yes, I was rebelling, but I can see now that there is a reason why people resist. And you must allow people to travel through them. I'm not saying I was wrong to spiral, but I don't think it's healthy to hamper someone's spirit to that extent and to tear them down to the point where they no longer feel like themselves. We, as individuals, must put the world to the test. You must push your limits in order to discover who you are and how you want to live.

That freedom was granted to others, and by others, I mean men. We believed male rockers were cooler because they arrived late to award presentations. Male pop artists were sleeping with a lot of ladies, which was fantastic. Kevin left me alone with two babies to go use marijuana and make a rap song called "Popozo," which is Portuguese slang for "big ass." Then he took them away from me, and he was named Dad of the Year by Details magazine. A paparazzo who hounded and tortured me for months sued me for $230,000 after I ran over his foot with my car one time while fleeing him. We came to an agreement, and I had to give him a large sum of money.

Growing up, I'd been eyeballed a lot. Since I was a youngster, I'd been scrutinised and had people tell me what they thought of my body. My methods of resistance included shaving my head and acting out. But, as a result of the conservatorship, I was made to believe that those days were over. I needed to grow my hair out and get in shape. I had to get to bed early and take whatever medication they prescribed.

If I thought getting ridiculed about my body in the news was awful, hearing it from my own father stung even more. He told me over and over that I looked obese and that I needed to do something about it. So I would put on my sweatpants and head to the gym every day. I'd dabble in some creative endeavours here and there, but my heart wasn't in it anymore. My passion for singing and dancing seemed almost comical at the time.

A child's soul is crushed when he or she believes they are never good enough. He'd instilled that message in me as a child, and he was still doing so even after I'd done so much.

I wanted to inform my father that you had ruined my life. You're making me work for you now. I'll do it, but damn me if I put my heart into it.

I turned into a robot. But not just any robot—a child-robot. I'd become so infantilized that I'd lost track of what made me feel like myself. I would refuse anything my father or mother commanded me to do. My feminine pride would not allow me to take it seriously. The conservatorship took away my womanhood and turned me into a child. Onstage, I became more of an entity than a person. They took away my ability to feel music in my bones and blood.

If they had allowed me to live my life, I know I would have followed my heart and gotten out of this the proper way.

Thirteen years passed while I felt like a shadow of myself. I feel terrible thinking about my father and his associates having power over my body and my money for so long.

Consider how many male artists blew all their money on gambling, and how many struggled with substance abuse or mental illness. Nobody attempted to take away their authority over their bodies or their money. What my family did to me was unjust.

The point was, even though I was purportedly unable to care for myself, I accomplished a lot.

I received over twenty honours in 2008, including the Cosmopolitan Ultimate Woman of the Year Award. I won three Moonmen at the VMAs, just one year after being criticised for my "Gimme More" performance. "Piece of Me" won every category in which it was nominated, including Video of the Year. I thanked God, my sons, and my followers for their support.

I found it almost amusing that I got those accolades for the record I made while apparently being so incapacitated that I had to be controlled by my family.

But, when I paused to think about it for a long time, it wasn't hilarious at all.

Chapter 30

I enjoyed the dry heat of Las Vegas. I liked how everyone trusted in luck and the dream. I had always enjoyed it there, even when Paris Hilton and I were kicking off our shoes and sprinting through casinos. But it felt like a lifetime ago.

In 2013, my residency began immediately after Christmas. The boys were aged seven and eight. It was a terrific gig at first.

It was exciting to be onstage in Vegas at first. And no one let me forget that my residency was a historic deal for the Strip. I was told that my show lured young people back to Sin City and transformed the scene of entertainment in Las Vegas for a new generation.

The fans gave me so much energy. I grew really good at doing the performance. I gained so much confidence, and for a while, everything was fine—as good as it could be while I was so tightly controlled. I began dating a TV producer named Charlie Ebersol. He seemed like marriage material to me: he took excellent care of himself. His family was close. I had feelings for him.

My father was not pleased. He knew what I ate and when I went to the potty. So when I started using energy supplements, he noticed that I had more energy onstage and was in better form than before. Charlie's programs appeared to be beneficial to me. But I believe my father began to suspect that I had a problem with those energy supplements, despite the fact that they were over-the-counter, not prescription. So he told me I had to get off them and sent me to rehab.

He gets to decide where I went and when I went. And going to treatment meant I wouldn't see my kids for a month. The only solace I had was knowing it was only for a month and that I'd be done with it.

He chose Malibu for me. We had to do boxing and other activities outside for hours a day that month because there was no gym.

Many of the people at the facility were major drug addicts. I was terrified to be there by myself. At the very least, I was allowed to have a security guard with whom I would have lunch every day.

When I got out, I went back to playing concerts in Vegas like nothing had happened. Part of it was because my father told me I needed to get back out there, and part of it was because I was still so lovely, so willing to please, so determined to do the right thing and be a good girl.

My father was always watching, no matter what I did. I couldn't drive a car. Everyone that came to my trailer had to sign waivers. Everything was extremely safe—so safe that I couldn't breathe.

Two years is a long time to go without eating what you want, especially when it's your body, your labour, and your soul that generate the money that everyone relies on. Two years of being denied french fries. It was quite demeaning to me.

A rigorous diet you've imposed on yourself is terrible enough. But it's made worse when you're denied food you crave. I felt as if my body was no longer mine. I'd go to the gym and feel so out of my mind with this trainer telling me to do things with my body that I felt chilly on the inside. I was afraid. To be honest, I was miserable.

And it didn't even work. The diet had the opposite impact that my father desired. I gained weight. Even if I wasn't eating as much, he made me feel unattractive and unworthy. Perhaps this is due to the power of your thoughts: whatever you think you are, you become. I was so exhausted by it all that I simply gave up. My mother seemed to agree with my father's plan for me.

It amazed me that so many people felt so at ease discussing my physique. It began when I was little. Whether it was strangers in the media or members of my own family, people seemed to regard my body as public property: something they could regulate, control, condemn, or use as a weapon. My body was strong enough to carry two children and agile enough to perform every rehearsed action flawlessly onstage. And now here I was, having every calorie tracked so that people might continue to profit from my body.

No one else seemed to think it was strange that my father would make all these rules for me and then go out and drink Jack and Cokes. My pals would come over and get their nails done at spas and drink expensive champagne. I was never allowed to go to spas. My family would remain in Destin, a lovely beach town in Florida, in an outrageously beautiful condo that I had purchased for them, and eat delicious food every night while I was famished and working.

I used to enjoy purchasing family homes and automobiles. But there came a time when they began to take things for granted, and the family didn't know that those things were available because I'm an artist. And because of how they treated me, I lost touch with my creativity for many years.

I was paid a weekly stipend of around $2,000 USD. If I desired a pair of footwear that my conservators didn't think I required, I'd be told no. Despite doing 248 concerts and selling over 900,000 tickets in Vegas. Each show paid hundreds of thousands of dollars.

On one of the few occasions that I went out to dinner with a buddy and others, including my dancers, I attempted to pick up the check for our entire party. The check was a thousand dollars because the group was so large, but I had wanted to take them out because I wanted them to know how much I appreciated how hard they worked. My purchase was rejected. I didn't have enough money in my "allowance" account to cover it.

Chapter 31

I enjoyed teaching dancing to youngsters at a studio once a month, which provided me with consolation and optimism during my time in Vegas. I instructed a class of forty children. Then, back in LA, I taught once every two months, not far from my house.

That was one of the most enjoyable experiences of my life. It was refreshing to be in a room with youngsters who were free of judgement. Everyone in the conservatory was continually judging anything I did. The excitement and trust of children my age—between five and twelve—is contagious. Their enthusiasm is wonderful. They are eager to learn. Being with children is completely healing for me.

I took a turn one day and accidentally hit a tiny little girl in the head with my hand.

"Baby! I'm very sorry!" I said.

I was so upset that I got down on my knees in front of her. I took a band off my finger, one of my favourite rings, and handed it to her, pleading for her forgiveness.

"Miss Britney, it's fine!" she exclaimed. "You didn't even hurt me."

I wanted to do everything I could to show her that I cared if she was in pain and that I would go to any length to make it up to her.

Wait a minute, I thought, looking up at her from my knees on the dance studio floor. Why are the people entrusted with my care by the state not half as concerned about my well-being as I am about this little girl's?

I made the decision to fight my way out of the conservatorship. In 2014, I went to court and requested that my father be drug-tested due to his drunkenness and erratic conduct. After all, he was in charge of both my money and my life. But my case was never heard. The judge simply did not pay attention.

What followed was a shady attempt to get my own counsel. I even referenced the conservatorship on a chat show in 2016, but that segment of the conversation never aired. Huh. How intriguing.

That sense of being trapped aided in the demise of my romantic life. Charlie and I became so arrogant after a dumb dispute that we stopped speaking to each other. It was the stupidest thing I'd ever done. I couldn't force myself to speak to him, and he was too proud to speak to me.

That's when I met Julia Michaels and Justin Tranter, two fantastic songwriters. We'd sit together and write everything. I was very enthusiastic about it. It was the one thing I really put my heart into during the conservatorship's thirteen years. I put forth a lot of effort on the tunes, which gave me confidence. You know how you can tell when you're good at something? You start doing something and think to yourself, "I've got this." Writing that record restored my confidence.

When I first saw Hesam Asghari on the set of my video for "Slumber Party," I knew I had to have him in my life. I was immediately smitten. The chemistry between us was incredible at first. We couldn't keep our hands from touching. He referred to me as his lioness.

The tabloids immediately began to report that he was cheating on me. We'd just been dating for two weeks! We remained together. My flame began to return to me.

My father then decided he needed to send me back to therapy since I'd snuck my over-the-counter energy tablets. He suspected I had a problem, but he showed mercy and said I could be an outpatient there as long as I went to Alcoholics Anonymous four times a week.

I hesitated at first, but the women I met there began to inspire me. As I listened to them recount their stories, I thought to myself, These women are brilliant. Their stories were genuinely extremely moving. In those meetings, I discovered a human connection that I had never experienced before in my life. And so, at first, I really liked it. However, some of the girls did not always appear. They may choose which meetings they wished to attend. I didn't have a choice in the issue. Friends I met there could go once a week, or they might go to a morning meeting one day and an evening meeting the following. I wasn't allowed to change anything.

Every week, no matter what, I had the same meetings at the same time.

But I was so good, I thought, remembering how hard I worked on those shows. I wasn't just good; I was fantastic. It was a sentence that came to mind again over the next few years as I considered how I had not only met but beyond the expectations that had been placed on me—and how unjust it was that I still wasn't free.

I'd worked so hard and stuck to the timetable they'd established for me—four weeks on, four weeks off. I used to do three two-hour shows a week when I was on. And, on or off, I adhered to the weekly plan they established for me: four AA meetings, two hours of treatment, and three hours of training every week, in addition to fan meet-and-greets and three gigs. I was exhausted. And I desired to be in charge of my own fate.

When one of my hairdressers saw my itinerary, she asked, "Oh, honey, what are you doing?" She was a mother figure to her two daughters. I really liked her.

"You think it's too much?" I inquired of her.

"It's more than too much," she admitted. "That's insane."

She leaned in, like if she had something important to tell me. "Listen," she instructed. "In order to be creative, you must make time in your schedule for play." Having that time to yourself helps to ground you. If you wish, you can just gaze at the wall. People require it."

What she'd said must have gotten back to my father, because the next day, someone else was doing my hair.

That hairstylist was never seen by me again.

Chapter 32

We girls have hair as performers. That's what real men want to see. They enjoy watching the long hair move. They want you to destroy it. They can tell you're having a good time if your hair is moving.

I donned tight wigs and danced in such a way that not a single hair on my head moved throughout the most depressing moments of my Las Vegas residency. Everyone who was earning money off of me wanted me to move my hair, and I was well aware of this—so I did everything but that.

When I look back, I realise how much of myself I withheld onstage, how much I punished everyone else by trying to hurt the individuals who held me captive—including my devoted followers and myself. But now I understand why I'd been sleepwalking for the previous thirteen years. I had been traumatised.

By holding back onstage, I was attempting to rebel in some manner, even if I was the only one who realised what was going on. As a result, I didn't toss my hair or flirt. I did the dances and sung the notes, but I wasn't as fired up as I had been in the past. My own kind of a factory slowdown was lowering my enthusiasm onstage.

As an artist, I was unable to achieve the sensation of freedom that I had previously experienced. And as artists, we have that freedom in who we are and what we do. Under the conservatorship, I was not free. I aspired to be a world-class woman. I couldn't be a woman while under guardianship.

Glory, on the other hand, was a different story. I became more enthusiastic about my performances when the Glory singles became available. I resumed wearing high heels. It came over most powerfully when I wasn't trying so hard and just allowed myself to transcend as a star onstage. And that's when I felt the audience really lift me up.

I have a hard time describing to folks who haven't been onstage what it's like to feel that current between your physical body and the bodies of other people in a room. Electricity is the only metaphor that truly works. You have an electrifying sensation. The energy flows out of you, through the crowd, and back into you in a loop. I'd had to be on autopilot for so long: the only current I could tap was whatever was inside of me that kept me moving.

I was swamped with health appointments at the start of the conservatorship. Doctor after doctor—probably twelve doctors a week—visiting my home. Nonetheless, when I requested an appointment to have my IUD removed, my father refused to allow me to go.

When the conservatorship was imposed, everything became monitored, with security guards stationed throughout. My entire existence shifted in ways that were maybe safer for me physiologically but were totally disastrous for my feeling of joy and creativity. "Oh, your life was saved!" several others exclaimed. But, no, not at all. It's all about how you look at it. It's all about perception. My music was my life, and the conservatory was lethal because it shattered my soul.

Prior to the conservatory, I had been in and out of recording studios. During my conservatory, a team of people kept track of when I went to the bathroom in the recording studio. I'm not exaggerating.

After the conservatorship, I discovered that my father and Robin at Lou Taylor's company, Tri Star, had been involved with the security company they hired, Black Box, in monitoring and reviewing calls and texts coming out of and going to my cell phone, including private texts with my boyfriend, my lawyer at the time, and my own children, and that my father had a bug installed in my home. At my own house! Everything was under their control.

I left home as a teenager because my family situation was so bad. All those times when I was a little girl and had to go out into the living room and say, "Shut up, Mama!" as my father lay passed out drunk in his chair—those times would come back to me when I woke up and stared at the ceiling, wondering how those people had come to be in charge again.

I vowed to do everything I could to get away in those calm periods in the middle of the night.

Chapter 33

That third year in Vegas, I felt something inside of me that I hadn't felt in a long, long time. I felt powerful. I realised I had to take action.

My body, heart, physique, and spiritual self could no longer accept the conservatorship once I began to return to myself. My small heart finally said, "I'm not going to stand for this."

My parents had convinced me for so long that I was the terrible guy, the insane one, and it had worked well in their advantage. It was a blow to my spirit. They put out my fire. For a decade, I devalued myself. But on the inside, I was yelling at them. You have to comprehend both the helplessness and the anger in that.

It irritated me to see my family drinking and having a good time after my gigs when I wasn't even allowed a taste of Jack and Coke. I knew I looked like a star onstage—I was wearing gorgeous tights and high heels—but why the fuck couldn't I sin in Sin City?

As I grew stronger and entered a new period of my womanhood, I began to look for models of how to use power for good. Reese Witherspoon was an excellent role model for me. She's sweet, pleasant, and quite intelligent.

I knew how to present myself. Putting up with that kind of schedule has made me tough. I had no choice but to be powerful, and I believe the audience sensed it. When you demand respect, it says a lot. It alters everything. So when I heard my conservators try to convince me yet again that I was stupid if I sought to decline a performance or find a way to give myself extra time off, I revolted. I told myself, "If you're trying to make me feel bad for saying no, I'm not going to fall for it again."

The residency was scheduled to conclude on December 31, 2017. I couldn't wait any longer. For starters, I had become tired of doing the same show week after week for years. I kept pleading for a remix or a new song to break up the boredom.

I'd begun to lose the excitement I'd felt when performing when I was younger. I no longer had the pure, unadulterated passion of singing that I had as a teen. Other people were now telling me what to sing and when to sing it. Nobody appeared to care what I wanted. The message I was getting was that their thoughts were important, but mine should be ignored. I was only there to entertain them and make them money.

It was such a waste of time. And, as a performer who has always taken great pride in her skills, I can't express how upset I was that they wouldn't even allow me to change up my show. In Vegas, we had weeks between each set of concerts. So much time was squandered. I wanted to give my audience something new and exciting by remixing my tunes. They wouldn't let me play my favourite songs, such as "Change Your Mind" or "Get Naked." They seemed to want to shame me rather than allow me to give my audience the best performance possible every night, which they deserved. Instead, I had to perform the same performance every week: the same routines, songs, and arrangements. I'd been performing shows like this for a long time. I was desperate to shake things up, to give my lovely, devoted audience something new and exciting. But all I could hear was "no."

When I pushed, they stated the best they could do was play one of my new songs in the background while I changed.

They pretended to be doing me a tremendous favour by playing my favourite new music while I was underground furiously changing costumes.

I felt so light and free when I was filming the visuals for Glory's singles. Glory brought up memories of how it felt to perform new stuff and how much I needed it. When I found out I'd be receiving the first-ever Radio Disney Icon Award the year after Glory was released, I thought to myself, This is fantastic! I'll take the boys and wear a gorgeous black dress, and we'll have a great time.

As I sat in the crowd, watching a mashup of my songs played, I was overcome with emotion. I was a ball of emotion by the time Jamie Lynn made a surprise appearance to sing "Till the World Ends" and gave me my prize.

I kept flashing back to the concert special I'd done for In the Zone while watching the show. It was an ABC program that had been remixed. I'd been practising for a week and had sung numerous new songs. They took really great pictures of me. I was like a kid. To be honest, it's some of my best work. A sensual performance of "... Baby One More Time" had a Cabaret feel to it, and for "Everytime," I wore a lovely white outfit. It was really breathtakingly lovely. It felt amazing to be at that point in my career, free and presenting my music in my own unique style, with complete creative control.

And, even though I was honoured by the performances, I was enraged as I accepted the Icon Award at the Radio Disney Music Awards. Three vocalists and my sister were making new arrangements—something I had pleaded for for thirteen years—having fun with my songs in ways I hadn't seen in hundreds of performances, and I couldn't help but smile.

Chapter 34

Cade, my friend and agent, used to contact me and say we should go on a road trip, and I'd be in the car before he finished telling me where we were going. If I wanted the volume turned up at one of my gigs, I'd gently request that the sound guy do so. If you irritated me, everyone would know about it. I felt like a badass. But in Vegas, I merely smiled and nodded and repeated the same show like a windup doll.

The fact that I'd have two vacations with my kids, like I did every year, was the only thing keeping me going. But the year Glory was released, I had to tour instead, which meant I couldn't go on vacation; I had to bring the kids on tour with me, which wasn't fun for anyone. So I really needed those holidays the next year. My team came in one night before a show and I flagged it for them: "Hey," I said, "I just wanted to give you a heads-up." This year, I really need those getaways."

Tradition is extremely important to me. My and my children's favourite activity was to travel to Maui, rent a boat, and sail out into the ocean. To be honest, it's for my mental health.

When I tried to compromise, the conversation quickly became heated. Finally, one of my team members stated, "If you don't go on tour, you will end up in court, because you have a contract." They were threatening me, I realised. And they were aware of how upsetting it was for me to be in court.

I eventually calmed down. I began to think that if it was only a few weeks, it wouldn't be so horrible. Then I could return and still enjoy some of the summer. We might simply go to Maui later.

This proved to be far too hopeful. The tour was a living nightmare. I'm sure the dancers felt it as well. My father's terms had us more bound than ever before. We had to give the security crew two hours' notice just to exit the room.

To make matters worse, I was still artistically inhibited, doing the same old thing. They were still not allowing me to rework my songs or change up the show. We could have adjusted the show and created something good, something new that would have felt new to the audience, as well as to me and the dancers. That was the one concession I requested, and they said no as usual. Because if I genuinely took charge of my show, people might realise that I don't need my father as a conservator. He seemed to enjoy making me feel "less than." It gave him authority.

I cried when I saw my pets when I arrived home since I'd missed them so much. I began to arrange a trip with the boys to make up for the time we'd lost. I explained to my team, "We'll give you three weeks off and then we have to start rehearsing for a new Vegas show."

"Three weeks?" I inquired. "I was supposed to have all summer!"

I'd detested the tour.

It was as if I had been told that the weekend would never come.

Chapter 35

I could already hear the screaming. Outside, hundreds of people had gathered. A large throng gathered outside the new Park MGM hotel in Las Vegas on an October day in 2018. Superfans wore similar outfits and waved flags with the word B on them. Onstage, dancers were wearing BRITNEY T-shirts. Announcers were live streaming their excitement to their followers. The laser lights flashed. A massive screen displayed scenes from my videos. Dance music was blasting. A parade passed past, with marchers screaming songs like "My loneliness is killing me!"

The lights were turned off.

"We are here to welcome the new queen of Vegas," Mario Lopez, who was on hand to host the event, shouted over the microphone.

The dramatic music began with a riff from "Toxic." Crazy lights flashed on the Park MGM, giving the impression that the structure was pulsing. Cue a medley of other tunes and images of a rocket ship, a helicopter, a circus large top, and a snake in Eden. Fire erupted from fire pits all around the stage! "... I climbed from the floor on a hydraulic lift, waving and smiling in a tight little black dress with star cutouts and tassels, my hair extra long and blond. Mario Lopez continued, "Ladies and gentlemen, Britney Spears!"

In my high heels, I strolled down the stairs to "Work Bitch" and signed a few autographs for admirers. But then I did something surprising.

I strolled right by the cameras.

I continued walking till I got into an SUV and drove away.

I remained silent. I did not deliver. You were undoubtedly wondering what just happened if you were watching.

What you didn't witness was my father and his staff attempting to bully me into announcing the show. I'd stated I didn't want to announce it because I didn't want to do it, as I'd been saying for months.

I had no concept of what overprotection was when I sang "Overprotected" so many years ago. I'd find out soon enough, because once I made it plain that I wasn't going to do Vegas anymore, my family had me leave.

Chapter 36

I was feeling very good as the holidays neared. Aside from my concern that my father was planning something, the women I'd met at AA made me feel strong and encouraged. They were bright, but they also had a lot of common sense, and I'd learned a lot from them about how to be an adult woman who navigated the world with honesty and boldness.

Hesam took me somewhere special for my birthday. I began making holiday plans, but my father insisted on taking the boys for Christmas. I'd have to see my father as well if I wanted to see them. "The boys don't want to be with you this year," my father stated when I resisted. They're returning to Louisiana with me and your mother, and that's the end of it."

"This is news to me," I continued, "but if they'd really rather be in Louisiana that week, I guess that's okay."

The Vegas event had not yet been cancelled. I was hiring new dancers and reviewing routines. I'd been working with all the dancers—new and old—at a rehearsal one day when one of the dancers who'd been with the show for four years did a move for us all. When I saw it, I winced; it looked quite difficult. "I don't want to do that one," I said. "It's too hard."

It didn't seem like much of a concern to me until my team and the directors abruptly disappeared into a room and locked the door. I had the impression that I had done something terrible, but I couldn't see how not wanting to complete one move in a routine could count as such. I mean, I was about five years older than when the previous residency began, and my physique had altered as well. What difference did it make if we switched things up?

From what I could gather, we'd all been having a good time. I suffer from social anxiety, therefore anything that makes me feel uneasy comes to me first. But everything seemed fine that day. I was laughing and conversing with the dancers. Some of the newcomers could do gainers, which is a standing back tuck in the future. They were fantastic! When I inquired whether I could learn it, one of them offered to tutor me. That is to say, we were both playing and conversing. Nothing seemed to be going wrong. But the way my crew had acted had me concerned that something was wrong.

A showy doctor, whom I had seen on TV and despised, came to my house against my will, sat me down, and assessed my cognitive ability for hours.

My father informed me that this doctor had determined that I had failed the tests: "She stated you failed. You must now visit a mental health centre. Something is seriously wrong with you. But don't worry, we've located a tiny recovery facility in Beverly Hills for you. It will only set you back $60,000 every month."

As I gathered my belongings, crying, I wondered how long I should pack and how long they'd make me remain. But I was assured that there was no way to find out. "Perhaps a month." Perhaps two months. Perhaps three months. It all depends on how effectively you perform and demonstrate your ability." The program was allegedly a "luxury" rehab that had designed a customised curriculum for me, so I wouldn't have to deal with other people.

"What if I don't go?" I inquired.

My father warned me that if I didn't go, I'd have to go to court and be humiliated. "We will make you look like a fucking idiot, and trust me, you will not win," he warned. It's better if I tell you to go than if a judge tells you."

It felt like blackmail and I was being gaslighted. They seemed to be attempting to kill me. In all those years, I had never stood up to my father; I had never said no to anyone. My no in that room that day truly irritated my father.

They made me go. I had no choice because they had my back to the wall. If you don't do it, this is what will happen to you, so we recommend you do it now.

But that didn't happen—getting it over with. Because I couldn't leave once I was there, no matter how much I begged.

They had me imprisoned against my will for months.

Chapter 37

The physicians whisked me away from my children, dogs, and home. I was unable to go outside. I couldn't operate a vehicle. I had to give blood once a week. I couldn't take a bath alone. I was unable to close the door to my room. Even as I was changing, I was being watched. At nine p.m., I had to go to bed. They watched TV with me in bed from eight to nine o'clock.

Every morning at eight o'clock, I had to get up. Every day was filled with meetings.

I sat in a chair for several hours a day, receiving obligatory therapy. I passed the time between appointments by peering out the window, watching automobiles pull up and drive away, so many cars delivering so many therapists, security guards, physicians, and nurses. What I think hurt me the most was watching all those people come and go while I was unable to go.

Everything that was occurring to me was for my own good, I was informed. But I felt abandoned in that environment, and even though everyone said they were there to help me, I never understood what my family expected from me. I completed all of my responsibilities. On weekends, my kids would come over for an hour. But I wouldn't be able to visit them if I didn't do what I was "supposed to do" throughout the week.

Cade was one of the few people that phoned me. Cade has always made me feel protected while also putting me in danger. The most amusing call I received the entire time was him FaceTiming me from a hospital in Texas to tell me about being bitten by a scorpion in his bed—in his bed. His leg ballooned to the size of a basketball.

"Are you serious right now?" Looking at his swollen leg on my phone, I murmured. It was shockingly bad. Cade's bad leg provided one of the few genuine distractions from what I was going through, and I'll be eternally thankful to him and that Texas scorpion.

The therapists interrogated me for hours on end, every day, seven days a week.

I'd been on Prozac for years, but in the hospital, they quickly yanked me off it and put me on lithium, a dangerous drug that makes you exceedingly slow and sleepy and that I didn't want or need. My sense of time began to shift, and I became bewildered. When I was on lithium, I had no idea where I was or even who I was. My mind wasn't working as it used to. It wasn't lost on me that my grandmother Jean, who eventually committed suicide, had been put on lithium in Mandeville.

Meanwhile, my long-term security crew treated me as if I were a criminal.

When it came time for blood draws, the tech would be surrounded by the nurse, a security guard, and my assistant.

Is it true that I was a cannibal? Is it true that I was a bank robber? Was I a savage beast? Why was I treated as if I was about to burn down the place and murder everyone?

They took my blood pressure three times a day, as if I were an eighty-year-old lady. They'd also take their time. Please make me sit. Obtain the cuff. Attach it gradually. Slowly increase the pressure... Every day, three times. I needed to move around to feel normal. As a dancer, movement was my existence. It fed my soul. I sought it and needed it. But they held me in that chair for what seemed like an eternity. I started to feel like I was being tortured ritually.

I was nervous in my feet, my heart, and my mind. I'd never be able to expend that much energy.

You know how when your body moves, it reminds you that you're alive? That was all I desired. And because I couldn't move, I began to worry whether I was already half-dead. I was devastated.

My ass grew so large from sitting in a chair for hours on end that none of my shorts fit anymore. I grew disconnected from my own body. I had horrible nightmares about running through a forest, dreams that were so real. Please wake up, please wake up, please wake up—I don't want it to be real, I'm sure this is only a dream.

If my intention in going there was to heal, that was not the result. I started picturing myself as a bird without wings. You know how, as a youngster, you'd run around with your arms spread and, with the wind rushing over your arms, you'd feel like you were flying for a split second? That was the sensation I desired. Instead, I felt like I was sinking into the soil every day.

In Beverly Hills, I completed the program on my own for two months. It was horrible, like I was in my own horror film. I enjoy watching scary movies. I saw The Conjuring. After six months at the treatment clinic, I'm not afraid of anything. I'm not afraid of anything now.

I'm probably the least afraid woman alive right now, but that doesn't make me strong; it makes me sad. I shouldn't be this powerful. Those months hardened me. I miss being what we used to call a sass ass in Kentwood. My sassiness was lost throughout my stay in the hospital. It shattered my spirit in so many ways.

I was moved after two months in one facility to another run by the same individuals, and this time I wasn't alone. Even though I used to enjoy being alone, it was honestly so much easier to be around other patients after two months in what felt like solitary confinement and on lithium. We spent the entire day together. Each of us was left alone in a separate room at night, and the doors shut with a pow sound.

I took a glance around my room. "I don't even have music playing," that's what I said.

I eventually discovered that she sometimes heard things that other people didn't, which terrified me.

An extremely attractive girl arrived and quickly became popular. It reminded me of high school, when she was the cheerleader and I was the depressed nerd. She skipped every meeting.

Despite the fact that many of the people there were insane, I liked the majority of them. One of the girls smoked skinny cigarettes, something I'd never seen before. Her cigarettes were as lovely as she was. I saw her father would see her on weekends. Meanwhile, my family had abandoned me in that location and gone about their lives.

"I know you see my cigarettes," the kind girl told me one day. "I bet you want to try one, don't you?" I had assumed she'd never ask. "Yeah," I replied.

So, with her and a few other girls, I smoked my first Capri cigarette.

There were a couple of people there who had eating disorders and were frighteningly thin. I didn't consume that much myself. I was shocked that I wasn't dying away, given how little I was eating and how much blood I was giving for all the tests.

God had to have been with me during that time. Three months into my incarceration, I began to suspect that my small heart, whatever it was that constituted me Britney, was no longer within my body. It was too much for me to handle alone, therefore something bigger must have carried me through.

I look at my survival and think, "That wasn't me; that was God."

Chapter 38

The most difficult thing was believing that I had to act fine in front of the physicians and visitors at all times. If I became agitated, it was interpreted as proof that I wasn't progressing. I was out of control and insane if I became upset and expressed myself.

It reminded me of how they used to test people to see whether they were witches in the earlier days. They were going to dump the woman into a pond. She was a witch and would be slain if she floated. If she drowned, she was innocent, so whatever. She was already dead, but I suppose they believed it was still worth knowing what kind of lady she'd been.

After a few months, I called my father and begged him to let me return home.

"I'm sorry," he replied, "the judge will have to figure out what she's going to do with you." Right now, it's up to the doctors. I'm afraid I'm powerless to assist you. I'm referring you to the physicians because I can't help you."

My father had sent me a pearl necklace and a beautiful handwritten message for Christmas before they put me in that situation. Why is he doing this, I wondered? What is his name?

What stung me the most was that he'd been stating in front of the cameras for years, whether it was when I did the "Work Bitch" video or when the conservatorship first began and we did the Circus Tour, that he was all about me and the guys.

She, like the rest of them, kept acting as if I was a threat in some way. This is going to sound weird, but it's the truth: I felt they were going to try to kill me.

I couldn't understand how Jamie Lynn and our father had such a close relationship. She was aware that I was seeking assistance from her and that he was following me. I believed she should have sided with me.

"Britney, I had three or four nightmares when you were at that centre," one of my companions who helped me change clothes every night in the underground changing room during my Vegas run later recounted. I'd awaken in the middle of the night. I had dreams that you committed suicide in that location. And I imagined that Robin, your so-called good assistant, called me and triumphantly declared, 'Yeah, she died in the location.'" My friend stated she was concerned about me the entire time.

I was battling to stay hopeful several weeks into my stay when one of the nurses, the only one who was genuine as hell, summoned me to her computer.

"Look at this," she pointed out.

I studied her computer, trying to make sense of what I was seeing. It was a group of women on a chat show discussing me and the conservatorship. One of them was dressed in a #FreeBritney T-shirt. The nurse also showed me footage of people asking whether I was being detained somewhere against my will, talking about how much my music meant to them and how they hated to think I was suffering now. They wished to assist.

And merely by doing so, they were able to assist. Everyone in the hospital was seeing everything the nurse was seeing. The doctor ultimately realised that people all around the world were wondering why I was still imprisoned. The story was all over the news.

In the same way that I believe I can sense how people are feeling in Nebraska, I believe my connection to my followers helped them instinctively recognize that I was in danger. No matter where we are in space, we are connected. Even if you're on the other side of the country or the planet, we're all connected on some level. Fans of mine seemed to know despite the fact that I had stated nothing about being confined online or in the press.

Seeing them marching through the streets, yelling "Free Britney!" was the most incredible sight I'd ever seen. I'm sure some folks laughed. "What kind of cause is this?" they asked, seeing the pink T-shirts with my name on them.

But I don't think people would have laughed if they truly realised what I was going through and the bond I have with my followers. The truth is that I was detained without my will. And I wished to believe that people cared whether I lived or died.

What do we have besides our bonds with one another? And what better way to connect than through music? Everyone who stood up for me helped me get through that difficult year, and the work they did helped me win my freedom.

I don't think people realised how much the #The FreeBritney movement meant something to me at first. It meant a lot to see individuals advocating for me during the court sessions near the end. But the first time it happened, it broke my heart because I was not okay at all. And the fact that my friends and fans realised what was going on and went out of their way to help me is a debt I'll never be able to repay. Thank you from the bottom of my heart if you stood up for me when I couldn't stand up for myself.

Chapter 39

I was overjoyed to be able to return to my house, my pets, and my children.

Guess who came to see me the first week I was back? My household.

"We're so proud of you, Britney!" exclaimed my father. "You accomplished it! We'd all like to come and be with you now." But by this stage, I could see right through his nonsense. "I can't wait to see your money—I mean, you!" he was truly saying.

So they arrived: my father, mother, and sister, together with her daughters, Maddie and Ivey.

I was nothing like myself. I was still on lithium, which muddled my sense of time. And I was terrified. It occurred to me that they were simply visiting to complete what they'd begun a few months before, to kill me for real. If that sounds paranoid, think about all I'd gone through up to this point—the ways they'd fooled and institutionalised me.

As a result, I played the game. They won't try to kill me again if I'm polite to them, I reasoned.

I hadn't gotten a hug from anyone in three and a half months.

How strong my young heart had to be makes me want to cry.

My family, on the other hand, came into my house as if nothing had happened. As if I hadn't just been through an absolutely excruciating experience in that location. "Oh, hey girl, what are you doing?" Jamie Lynn stated cheerfully.

She'd finally found her groove. I was delighted for her. At the same time, I didn't want to be near it just now.

"Oh my God, I have this really great idea for me and you!" She'd say as I rested, almost drowsy, on the countertop after returning from yet another meeting. "Get this—a sister talk show!" Every time she spoke, she had a new plan. A comedy! A romantic comedy!

She spoke for what seemed like hours at a time, as I sat on the floor and listened. And the phrase that kept ringing in my head was What in the world is going on?

When my family departed my house after that dreadful visit, I realised how much I'd gone through. And all I was left with was a blind hatred. They'd chastised me. For what purpose? For having supported them since I was a child?

How had I avoided killing myself there, putting myself out of my suffering like a lame horse? Almost anyone else in my situation, I believe, would have done the same.

I sobbed as I remembered how close I came to doing just that. Then something happened to shake me out of my trance.

My father was battling with Sean Preston, who was thirteen at the time, that August. My kid went to lock himself in a bedroom to halt the fight, and my father shook him and broke down the door. Kevin filed a police report, and my father was denied access to the children.

I knew I had to summon one more round of strength in order to battle one more time. It had been a long journey. Of regaining faith and then losing it again. Being knocked down and rising again. Of chasing after freedom just to have it slip right out of my grasp.

If I was strong enough to withstand everything, I could take a chance and ask God for just a little bit more. I was going to demand the end of the conservatorship with every fibre of my motherfucking being.

Because I didn't want those folks to control my life any longer. I didn't want them even in my own kitchen.

I didn't want them to have the authority to keep me from my children, my house, my pets, or my automobile ever again.

If I can manifest anything, I reasoned, why not an end to this?

Chapter 40

The first step toward regaining my freedom was for people to realise that I was still a real person, which I knew I could do by sharing more of my life on social media. I began trying on new clothing and posting photos of myself wearing them on Instagram. It was a lot of fun for me. Even though some people felt it was strange, I didn't mind. It feels amazing to be in complete control of the clothes and the camera after being sexualized your entire life.

I tried to reconnect with my creativity by following visual and musical artists on Instagram. I stumbled upon a guy who was making strange videos, one of which was simply a baby-pink screen with a white tiger with pink stripes roaming over it. Seeing that, I felt compelled to make something of my own, so I began experimenting with a tune. I started it out with the sound of a baby laughing. It struck me as unusual.

"Don't put a baby laughing in it!" Hesam advised.

I heeded his advice and removed it, but then another account I follow posted a video of a baby giggling, and I was jealous. That is something I should have done! I pondered. That scary laughing infant should have been my speciality!

Artists are strange, you know?

There were many people in the industry who thought I was insane at the time. At some point, I'd rather be "crazy" and be allowed to make whatever I want than "a good sport" and do what everyone tells me to do without being able to express myself. And I wanted to demonstrate my existence on Instagram.

I also found myself laughing more, thanks to Amy Schumer, Kevin Hart, Sebastian Maniscalco, and Jo Koy. I admired their humour and brilliance, and how they utilise language to get under people's skin and make them laugh. That's a wonderful present. Hearing people use their voices and being themselves encouraged me that I could do the same when I uploaded videos for social media or even just in a description. Humour allowed me to avoid becoming overtaken by bitterness.

I've always appreciated those with sharp wits in the entertainment sector. Laughter is the best medicine.

Those may laugh because the things I share are innocent or strange, or because I can be harsh when discussing those who have wounded me. Perhaps there has been a feminist awakening. I guess what I'm saying is that the mystery of who the actual me is works in my favour—no one knows!

My children occasionally make fun of me, which I don't mind.

They've always helped me shift my outlook on life. They've always seen things differently since they were children, and they're both quite creative. Sean Preston is an academic genius—he is extremely intelligent. Jayden has such a natural talent for the piano that it gives me chills.

They used to join me for excellent dinners two or three nights a week before the pandemic. They were continuously showing me their great creations and telling me what they were enthused about.

"Mom, check out this painting I made!" one of them would exclaim. When I told them what I observed, they'd remark, "Yeah, but now, Mom, look at it like this." And I'd notice even more in what they'd created. I admire them for their depth and character, as much as their talent and goodness.

Everything was just starting to make sense again as we entered a new decade.

Then COVID struck.

During the first few months of lockdown, I became even more of a homebody than I was before. I sat in my room for days, weeks, listening to self-help CDs, staring at the wall, or crafting jewellery, bored out of my mind. After I'd exhausted my supply of self-help audiobooks, I went on to storytelling audiobooks, anything labelled "Imagination"—especially anything with a British narrator.

However, out in the world, my father's security crew continued to enforce the regulations. I was on the beach one day when I removed my mask. Security came over to chastise me. I was chastised and grounded for several weeks.

I didn't have Hesam with me because of the quarantines and his job schedule.

I was so lonely that I started missing my family.

I called my mother and said, "I want to see you guys."

"We're shopping right now," she explained. I have to leave! We'll get back to you later."

They then didn't.

In Louisiana, the lockdown rules were different, and they were always out and about.

I eventually gave up on calling them and travelled to Louisiana to visit them. They appeared so liberated there.

Why was I still talking to them? I'm not certain. Why do we continue to be in dysfunctional relationships? For one thing, I was still afraid of them, and I wanted to be friendly to them. My father was still legally my father, as he was quick to emphasise out—though I hoped not for long.

During this time with my family, I discovered that while I was in the mental health facility, they'd thrown away a lot of what I'd kept at my mother's house. My Madame Alexander dolls from childhood were all gone. So were they.

Chapter 41

The court-appointed lawyer who had been with me for thirteen years had never been of much assistance, but during the epidemic, I began to wonder whether I could perhaps utilise him to my advantage. I started talking to him twice a week, like a prayer, simply to think about my possibilities. Was he working for me, my father, or Lou?

I'd say to myself as he talked around the subject, "You don't seem to believe in what I know: I know where I'm going with this." I'll go all the way to the end. I can tell you're not going to finish this.

Finally, I reached a tipping point. There was nothing else he could do for me. I had to take charge.

I had kept quiet about the whole thing in public, but I was praying in my brain for it to end. I'm talking about genuine prayer...

So, on the evening of June 22, 2021, I dialled 911 from my residence in California to report my father for conservatorship abuse.

The period in limbo between when I began pushing aggressively to stop the conservatorship and when it finally ended was difficult. I had no idea how things would turn out. Meanwhile, I couldn't say no to my father or make my own way, and it seemed like there was another documentary on me on yet another streaming service every day. This is what I was thinking when I found out my sister was writing a book.

My father still had influence over me. I was powerless to defend myself. I wanted to blow up.

It was difficult to see the documentaries about me. I appreciate that everyone's intentions were good, but I was offended when some old acquaintances spoke to filmmakers without first contacting me. I was astounded that someone I trusted had gone on camera. I couldn't comprehend how people could gossip about me behind my back. If that had been me, I would have called my friend to verify if it was okay to mention her.

There was a lot of speculation about what I could have thought or felt.

Chapter 42

"Miss Spears?" You are welcome to address me."

The voice broke through the phone line. I was sitting in my living room. It was a typical Los Angeles July afternoon.

On June 23, 2021, I was finally scheduled to testify in a Los Angeles probate court on the conservatorship. And I knew the entire world was watching. I'd been training for days, but now that the big moment had arrived, the stakes were too high. Not least because I knew that because I had requested that this hearing be open to the public, millions of people would be listening to my voice as soon as I finished speaking.

My own voice. It was everywhere, all over the world—on the radio, television, and the internet—but it had suppressed so many aspects of me. My voice had been used so many times for and against me that I was frightened no one would recognize it now if I spoke freely. What if they labelled me insane? What if they found out I was lying? What if I said the wrong thing and everything went wrong? I had so many different variants of this statement. I'd tried a million different ways to get it perfect, to say what I needed to say, but suddenly I was so frightened.

And then, in the midst of my fear, I remembered that there were still things I could cling to: My want for others to comprehend what I'd been through. My belief that everything may change. My idea that I had a right to be happy. My conviction that I deserved to be free.

This deep and genuine sense that the lady within me was still strong enough to fight for what was right.

I raised my eyes to Hesam, who was sitting on the couch next to me. He gripped my hand.

So, for the first time in what seemed like an eternity, I began to share my experience.

"I've lied and told the whole world I'm fine and happy," I told the court. It's a shame. I reasoned that if I just repeated it enough times, I may become pleased, because I've been in denial... But now I'm going to tell you the truth, okay? I'm not pleased. I'm having trouble sleeping. I'm insanely enraged. I'm also depressed. Every day, I cry."

"I don't even drink alcohol," I continued. Given what they've done to my heart, I should consume alcohol."

"I wish I could stay on the phone with you forever," I continued, "because when I get off the phone with you, all I hear are these nos." And then, all of a sudden, I feel ganged up on, bullied, left out, and alone. And I'm sick of being alone. By having a child, a family, or any of those things, I ought to have the same rights as everybody else, if not more. That's all I had to say to you. And thank you for allowing me to speak to you today."

I was gasping for air. It was the first opportunity I'd had to speak publicly in a long time, and a flood of emotions erupted. I waited to hear the judge's response. I hoped to get a sense of where her mind was at.

"I just want to tell you that I certainly am sensitive to everything that you said and how you're feeling," she told me. "I know that it took a lot of courage for you to say everything you have to say today, and I want to let you know that the court does appreciate your coming on the line and sharing how you're feeling."

That gave me a sense of relief, as if I'd finally been heard after thirteen years.

I've always worked quite hard. For a long time, I put up with being restrained. But my relatives went too far when they placed me in that facility.

I was handled as if I were a criminal. And they made me believe I deserved it. They made me lose sight of my own worth and value.

The worst thing they did, in my opinion, was to make me doubt my faith. I've never held firm religious beliefs. I just had a feeling there was something bigger than myself. I ceased believing in God for a spell while under their control. When it came time to end the conservatorship, however, I knew one thing: you can't fuck with a woman who knows how to pray. Pray fervently. I did nothing except pray.

Chapter 43

For the previous thirteen years, I had been duped. The entire world knew I needed a new lawyer, and I eventually acknowledged it as well. It was time for me to reclaim control of my own life.

I asked my social media team and my friend Cade for assistance in locating one. This is when I brought in Mathew Rosengart, who was fantastic. He had a number of renowned clients, including Steven Spielberg and Keanu Reeves, and a lot of expertise with high-profile, tough cases as a notable former federal prosecutor now with a large legal firm. We spoke on the phone numerous times before meeting in my pool home in early July. I felt like I was getting closer to the end once Mathew was in my corner. Something had to give. It couldn't remain stationary. But, because we were dealing with the legal system, we had to do a lot of waiting and thinking.

He was shocked that I'd been refused access to a lawyer for so long. He claimed that even the most heinous criminals get to choose their own lawyers, and he detested bullying. I was relieved because I saw my father, Lou, and Robin as bullies who needed to be removed from my life.

Mathew stated that he would first go to court and file a motion to remove my father as conservator, and then it would be easier to try to cancel the entire conservatorship. Just a few weeks later, on July 26, he filed paperwork to remove my father from that position. My father was removed as my conservator after a lengthy court hearing on September 29. Before Mathew could even phone me after court, it was all over the press.

I felt a wave of relief go over me. The man who had terrified me as a child and ruled over me as an adult, who had done more than anybody else to erode my self-esteem, was no longer in charge of my life.

With my father gone, Mathew told me we had momentum, and he petitioned for the conservatorship to be lifted entirely.

In November, I was at a Tahiti resort when Mathew called to tell me that I was no longer in conservatorship. He'd promised me before I left for the vacation that one day soon I'd be able to wake up as a free woman for the first time in thirteen years. Still, I couldn't believe it when he contacted me as soon as he got out of court and told me everything was done. I was liberated.

Despite the fact that his approach had led to our win, he insisted that I take credit for what had occurred. He claimed that by testifying, I had emancipated myself and most likely benefited other persons in unfair conservatorships. After having my father take credit for everything I accomplished for so long, hearing this man say that I'd made a difference in my own life meant everything.

I've been attempting to reconstruct my life day by day in the months after that phone call. I'm trying to learn how to take care of myself while also having fun.

I got to do something I'd wanted to do for years while on vacation in Cancun: jet skiing. The last time I'd gone Jet Skiing was in Miami with the boys, when I went too fast attempting to keep up with them. On a Jet Ski, the kids are borderline deadly! They go at high speeds and perform jumps. Riding over the waves behind them, I crashed hard—boom, boom, boom—and fell down, tumbling out and injuring my arm.

Not wishing to go through that again, I had my assistant drive me instead in May 2022. I've discovered that having someone drive you is far superior. This time, I could feel the force of the engine, enjoy being out on the clear blue lake, and go as fast as I wanted.

That's what I'm doing now: trying to have fun but still being kind to myself and taking things at my own pace. And, for the first time in a long time, I'm giving myself permission to trust again.

I listen to music every day. I feel entirely free, completely at ease, and completely pleased when I stroll about my house singing. I don't care whether I sound perfect or not. Singing, like exercise or prayer, makes me feel confident and strong. (Keep in mind that your tongue is your sword.) Anything that raises your heart rate is beneficial. Music is that, plus a link to God. That is the location of my heart.

I used to adore going to a Malibu studio when I had full-time access to one. I wrote six songs in one day. When I'm doing music for me, it's at its purest. I thought about getting a studio again and simply messing around, but I hadn't thought about recording in a long time.

I changed my mind when I was offered to record a song with Sir Elton John, a musician I've respected my entire life. He's one of my favourite artists of all time. I met him at an Oscars party about a decade ago and we hit it off right away. And now he's reached out with the sweetest video message, asking if I'd like to collaborate on one of his most renowned songs. "Hold Me Closer" would be a modernised duet version of his smash "Tiny Dancer," with elements from a couple of his other songs thrown in for good measure.

I felt very honoured. Elton John, like me, has been through a lot in public. It has given him tremendous sympathy. What a stunning man on every level.

To make the cooperation even more significant, as a child, I used to listen to "Tiny Dancer" in the vehicle on my way to and from dance and gymnastics classes in Louisiana.

Sir Elton was gracious and made me feel at ease. I went to the producer's home studio in Beverly Hills after we agreed on a recording date.

The studio was located in the house's basement. I'd never seen anything like it: a completely open studio with guitars, pianos, soundboards, and music equipment. I was scared since it would be the first time in six years that the world would hear my singing voice on anything fresh, but I believed in the song and in myself, so I went for it.

I took a step forward in front of the microphone, increased the tempo, and began to sing. We were finished after a few hours. On one of my favourite tracks, I recorded a duet with one of my favourite artists. In the weeks preceding up to the release, I was excited, apprehensive, and emotional.

Before the conservatory, when I went onstage, everyone looked to me for the signal that it was time to begin the performance. I'd raise my pointer finger and say, "Let's go." I was always forced to wait for everyone else during the conservatorship. I was told, "We'll let you know when we're ready." They didn't seem to regard me as having any worth. I despised it.

The conservatorship had taught me to be nearly too vulnerable, too afraid. That was the cost of the conservatorship. They took a lot of my femininity, my sword, my core, my voice, and my capacity to say "Fuck you." And I realise that sounds horrible, but there is something important here. Don't underestimate your strength.

"Hold Me Closer" will be released on August 26, 2022. We were number one in forty nations by August 27. My first number one and longest-charting single in nearly a decade. And only on my terms. Complete command. Fans stated I sounded wonderful on the music. It's daunting to share your work with the rest of the world. In my experience, however, it is always worthwhile. It was an incredible pleasure to record "Hold Me Closer" and release it into the world. It didn't feel good; it felt fantastic.

Moving further in my music career is not my priority right now. Now is the moment for me to strive to organise my spiritual life, to pay attention to the details, and to slow down. It's time for me to stop being someone that other people want and start being myself.

I've grown to appreciate my alone time as I've become older. Being an entertainer was amazing, but my desire to amuse in front of a live audience has waned over the previous five years. I now do it for myself. When I'm alone, I feel closer to God.

I'm no saint, but I know who God is.

I need to do some soul-searching. It will be a long process. I'm already having fun with it. Change is beneficial. We always pray together, Hesam and I. I look up to him because of his consistency in working out, being a decent man, being healthy, taking care of me, and teaching me how we can take care of each other.

I'm grateful to him for being such an influence. The conclusion of the conservatorship was ideal for our relationship; we were allowed to start a new life together, free of restrictions, and marry. Our wedding was a lovely celebration of how far we'd come together and how much we desired for each other's happiness.

I was overcome with emotions the day the conservatorship ended: astonishment, relief, elation, sadness, and joy.

I felt deceived by my father and, unfortunately, by the rest of my family as well. My sister and I should have found solace in one other, but that hasn't happened. She was writing a book about the conservatorship while I was fighting it and getting a lot of press attention. She hurriedly told me lurid things, many of which were unpleasant and ridiculous. I was quite disappointed.

Shouldn't sisters be free to express their fear or vulnerability to one another without it being used as evidence of instability later on?

I couldn't get the feeling that she had no idea what I'd been through.

She seemed to think it was easy for me because I had achieved so much renown so young, and she blamed me for my success and everything that came with it.

Jamie Lynn was plainly suffering in our family home as well. She grew up as a divorced child, whereas I did not. She didn't appear to get a lot of parenting, and I know it was difficult for her to try to sing and act and find her own way in the world in the shadow of a sibling who received not only the majority of the family's attention, but also a lot of the world's. For all of these reasons, my heart goes out to her.

But I don't think she realises how painfully poor we were before she was born. She wasn't helpless in the face of our father because of the money I brought to the family, as my mother and I were in the 1980s. When you have nothing, the pain is heightened by your inability to flee. My mother and I were forced to see the depravity and brutality without believing there was anywhere else to go.

She'll always be my sister, and I adore her and her lovely family. I wish them nothing but the best. She's gone through a lot, including a teen pregnancy, divorce, and a near-fatal accident with her daughter. She's mentioned the agony of growing up in my shadow. I'm trying to be more compassionate than angry toward her and everyone else who has hurt me. It is not simple.

June has told me in dreams that he knows he wounded my father, who then hurt me. I could feel his affection and see how he'd changed on the other side. I hope to be able to feel better about the rest of my family one day.

My rage has manifested physically, particularly in the form of migraine migraines.

When I get them, I don't want to go to the doctor since being sent from one doctor to the next for so long has given me a phobia of them. As a result, I handle things myself. When it comes to migraines, I don't like to talk about them because I'm afraid it will make them worse.

I can't go into the light and I can't move when I have one. In the dark, I maintain complete stillness. Any light causes my head to throb and makes me feel dizzy—it's that awful. I'll be sleeping for a day and a half. I'd never had a headache in my life until recently. When my brother complained about his headaches, I assumed he was exaggerating how awful they were. I'm sorry I ever said anything to cast doubt on him.

A migraine is worse than stomach sickness in my opinion. With a bug, you can still think clearly. Your mind can assist you decide what you want to do and what movies to watch. When you get a migraine, however, you are unable to function since your brain is absent. Migraines are only one aspect of the physical and mental trauma I've suffered since being released from conservatorship. I don't believe my family realises the extent of their actions.

For thirteen years, I couldn't eat what I wanted, drive, spend my money as I wanted, or even drink coffee.

The freedom to do anything I want has restored my femininity. In my forties, I'm experiencing things for the first time. I feel like the lady in me has been suppressed for far too long.

I'm finally roaring back to life. I might be able to sin in Sin City as well.

Chapter 44

For the first time in many years, I've begun to appreciate the benefits of being an adult woman. I feel like I've been underwater for a long time, only sometimes swimming to the surface to gulp for oxygen and a bite to eat. When I regained my freedom, it was my cue to go onto dry land—and to take vacations, sip a cocktail, drive my car, visit a resort, or gaze out at the ocean whenever I wanted.

I've been taking things day by day and trying to be grateful for the little things. I'm grateful that my father is no longer in my life. I no longer have to be afraid of him. If I gain weight, it'll be a relief to know that no one will be screaming at me, "You need to pick it up!" I got to eat chocolate once more.

My body got strong and my fire returned as soon as my father was no longer present to force me to consume what he wanted me to eat. I felt more confident, and I began to like how I looked again. On Instagram, I enjoy dressing up.

Many people don't understand why I enjoy photographing myself naked or in new clothes. But I think if they'd been shot hundreds of times by other people, prodded and positioned for other people's approval, they'd realise that I get a lot of delight from posing the way I feel sexy and taking my own picture, doing anything I want with it. I was born nude into this world, and I truly believe the weight of the world has been placed on my shoulders. I wanted to see myself as lighter and more liberated. I had my entire life in front of me as a baby, and that's how I feel now, like a blank slate.

I truly believe I have been reincarnated. I adore the sense of the voice leaving my body and bouncing back at me when I sing while I move around at home, exactly like I did when I was a little kid. I'm rediscovering why I wanted to sing in the first place. That sensation is sacred to me. I do it for me and no one else.

I'm constantly asked when I'm going to put on another concert. I'll admit that I'm stumped by that question. I'm dancing and singing like I used to when I was younger, not for the benefit of my family or to get something, but for myself and my real enjoyment of it.

Only now do I feel like I'm regaining my confidence in other people and in God. I know what makes me happy and joyful. I attempt to dwell on the places and concepts that allow me to have that experience. Beautiful places, my sons, my husband, my friends, and my pets are all things I enjoy. I adore my followers.

When it comes to admirers, they occasionally inquire about my special bond with the gay community.

It's all about love—unconditional love—for me. My gay buddies were constantly protective of me, perhaps because they understood I was somewhat naïve. Not stupid, but far too nice. And I believe many of the gay men around me were supportive. I could even feel it onstage while they were standing next to me. If I didn't think I gave my greatest performance, I could count on my friends to notice and yet exclaim, "You did so good!" That type of affection means the world to me.

My favourite nights were when I went out with my dancers. We went to a homosexual bar in Europe once, and I felt like everyone on the dance floor was so tall. I enjoyed the club's excellent electro dance music. I danced until six o'clock in the morning and it felt like two seconds. My heart was racing. It was a spiritual experience to be with individuals who I could feel loved me unreservedly, similar to the mystical time in Arizona. It doesn't matter what you do, say, or who you know when you have pals like that. That is genuine love.

I recall going to a showcase in Italy when several drag artists sang my tunes. It was incredible. The painters were stunning. They were completely immersed in the moment, and I could tell they enjoyed performing. They had a lot of passion and determination, which I admire.

When I was released from the conservatorship, I was able to visit the two holiday spots that I had missed, Maui and Cancun. I swam in the ocean, sat in the sun, played with Sawyer, my new puppy, and went on boat excursions with Hesam. I read extensively before writing this book. I discovered I was pregnant while on the road. I'd desired another child for a long time. Hesam and I had wanted to create our own family for a long time. I admire him for his stability. I adore the fact that he does not even drink. He is a divine gift. And learning that Chris and I were expecting our first child together made me ecstatic.

I, too, was terrified. I was depressed during my pregnancy with Sean Preston and Jayden. This pregnancy was similar in many ways—I was a little unwell and liked food and sex—and I worried if the sadness would return as well. I did notice that I was moving a little slower. I prefer to be up and about. But because my life was so much better and I had so much support, I was convinced I could get through it.

I miscarried before the end of my first trimester. I'd been so excited to be pregnant that I'd informed everyone, which meant I had to un-tell everyone. "It is with great sadness that we must inform you that we have lost our miracle baby early in the pregnancy," we wrote on Instagram. This is a difficult time for any parent. Perhaps we should have waited until we were farther along before announcing. We were, nonetheless, overjoyed to convey the good news. Our strength comes from our affection for one another. We will continue to try to grow our wonderful family. We appreciate all of your assistance. We respectfully request privacy during this difficult time."

I was saddened by the loss of the baby. But, once again, music assisted me in gaining understanding and perspective. Every song I sing or dance to allows me to convey a different story and provides a fresh avenue for me to escape. Listening to music on my phone helps me deal with the anger and despair that come with being an adult.

I try not to worry about my family too much these days, but I'm curious what they'll think of this book. Because I was suppressed for thirteen years, I wonder if they've ever thought, Maybe she's right, when they see me speaking out. I believe they have a guilty conscience, that they realise deep down that what they did to me was wrong.

All those years of doing what I was told and being treated in a specific way have taught me what kinds of people I want to be around and who I don't. Much of the media has been unkind to me, and this hasn't changed just because I'm no longer in conservatorship. There has been much conjecture regarding how I am doing. I know my fans are concerned. I am now free. I'm simply being myself and attempting to mend. I can finally do what I want, when I want. And I don't take anything for granted.

On social media, freedom means being foolish and ridiculous. Freedom means being able to take a break from Instagram without having to contact 911. Freedom entails the ability to make mistakes and learn from them. I'm free because I don't have to perform for anyone, on or offstage. Freedom allows me to be as delightfully flawed as everyone else. And freedom entails the opportunity and right to seek joy in my own way, on my own terms.

It took a long time and a great deal of effort for me to feel ready to relate my tale. I hope it inspires people and touches their hearts in some way. Since I've been free, I've had to create an entirely new identity. I've had to remind myself, "Wait a minute, this is who I was—someone passive and pleasing." A girl. And this is who I am now: someone strong and self-assured. A lady.

I had grandiose fantasies when I was a little child, laying on the warm rocks in my neighbour's garden. I felt composed and in command. I was confident that I could make my aspirations come true. I didn't always have the power to make the world seem the way I wanted it to for a long time, but I do now in many ways. I can't alter the past, but I no longer have to feel lonely or afraid. I've gone through a lot since I was a kid wandering the Louisiana woods. I've written music, toured the world, become a mother, found and lost love, and found it again. I hadn't been genuinely present in my own life, in my own strength, in my womanhood in a long time. But now I'm here.